Table of Cc

MW00807673

So, You've Been Called a Narcissist, Now What?

Doing the Work to End Patterns of Narcissism and Emotional Abuse

Dr. David B. Hawkins

Dr. John Hudson

The characters and events portrayed in this book are fictitious. Any similarity to real persons, living or dead, is coincidental and not intended by the author.

No part of this book may be reproduced, stored in a retrieval system, or transmitted in any form or by any means, electronic, mechanical, photocopying, recording, or otherwise, without express written permission of the publisher.

Cover design by: Katie Buckley
Printed in the United States of America.

ISBN- 979-8-99141-250-6

EAI Publishing

Acknowledgments / Dedication – Dr. David B. Hawkins

Our phones ring off the hook with requests for help. Women call in profound distress and discouragement, asking if we can help with years of narcissistic and emotional abuse.

Men also call. Their calls are quite different, however. They complain mightily about being called "an emotional abuser, a Narcissist," and desperately want counseling to be "a two way street."

It's not a two-way street. At least not yet.

In this context, Dr. John Hudson, my esteemed colleague, and I decided we needed to help men make the emotional shift from victim to victor, from blame-shifting to ownership, from complaining to courageously facing their issues, cleaning their side of the street, before expecting anything from their mates. It's tough work.

It was with this need in mind that I flew to Kansas City to brainstorm with Dr. John---and the book was born.

"So You've Been Called a Narcissist, Now What?: Doing the Work to Heal from Narcissism and Emotional Abuse."

Dr. Hudson and I spent hours discussing, brainstorming, and agreeing on the book outline, and the rest is history. Dr. Hudson and I wrote the book—thank you Dr. Hudson--- while my wife, Christie, tirelessly edited and made our writing efforts clear, compelling, and provocative. Thank you, Christie.

Katie, simultaneously, did her magic at creating a beautiful and engaging book cover, while she and Wendi worked on formatting, layout, and design. Esther, meanwhile, used her magic to prepare the market for this much-needed book. Whew! It takes a team to make a book. Thank you to my dedicated team of friends and colleagues.

We are very excited about this book. Both men and women need it. There IS hope for healing beyond narcissistic and emotional abuse.

Acknowledgments/Dedication -Dr. John Hudson

I must acknowledge all my past, present, and future Clients and all the challenges presented by and through them. Without their inspiration, we might not have seen and addressed the need to endeavor in the task. This project was born out of need – out of necessity. Many of our Clients – the men – asked: "Where is the book for me/for us?" There are many books written to the victims of abuse. However, we clearly got the message – the men demanded we write the book for them. A couple of phone conversations and a brainstorming weekend – we pulled together the vision and plan! When Dr. Hawkins invited me to collaborate on this project – I was thrilled! Noting Dr. Hawkins' extensive background, I was humbled he would ask me to partner on such an important undertaking. We had to get this right – for our clients! To Dr. David Hawkins, thank you for having the vision and courage to invite me along on this challenging and life-changing ride! Your dedication to our team, our clients, and the Marriage Recovery Center and Emotional Abuse Institute's vision is vibrant and clear.

I have learned from so many mentors and colleagues over these many years, that there are too many to list individually – however, you know who you are – thank you! Your motivation and commitment to serving many who struggle to help themselves have driven me to learn, develop skills, and serve with humility. You all sacrifice – daily – for your Clients and I so appreciate how much you've instilled this in me.

Most importantly, I am most grateful for the loving support of my wife, Lori, throughout our many years together. You give so much to "us" and encourage me tirelessly – thank you! I will love you forever and always.

You've Been Called You a Narcissist, Now What?

Prelude: Dr. David B. Hawkins

What the....? I am not a Narcissist. I am the same person she married. I haven't changed. Why am I suddenly the bad guy? I'm sick of it.

She keeps throwing all these terms at me -narcissist, gaslighting, blame-shifting. Everything's about me. It's all about how bad I am, how I'm making her crazy. How about how she makes me feel? How about me feeling just as crazy?

I'd like to tell her what I'm feeling, but you can only imagine how that would land. It's all about her feelings, her sadness, her frustration, her anger. It's all about her, and if I try and stop her to tell her how I feel, she accuses me of not listening to her and having to be the one with the bigger hurt.

She says she can't live with me the way I am, and if I don't get help, she's done.

Sound familiar?

I'm betting it does because I talk to men every day who feel this way. I'm Dr. David Hawkins, Director of The Marriage Recovery Center and Emotional Abuse Institute and the men I work with are totally confused, totally frustrated and they don't know how they got to where they are in their marriages. Their wives are reading books, watching videos, and listening to podcasts about Narcissistic men, and now their wives are making demands for change.

Men tell me there are a boatload of books available to help women, but none to help them. In fact, so many men complain about the lack of material available for men, my colleague and coauthor Dr, John Hudson and I decided to write this book.

Let's face facts. What you're doing isn't working. We get it. You're angry, hurt, and very confused. Out of that confusion you say and do things that only make matters worse. We can help.

Taking a Step Back

Chapter One: Dr. David B. Hawkins

So, why are you reading this book? Is it because your life is not working? Have you faced criticisms and ultimatums again and again, been accused of being selfish, narcissistic, and emotionally abusive, and can't ignore these complaints any longer?

These complaints and criticisms haven't come from nowhere, of course. They have arisen from an issue known as narcissism, for which the simplest definition is profound selfishness. The complaints have more than likely arisen because of emotional abuse, which is a result of narcissism and profound selfishness and involves the devaluing of another person, over and over.

You've heard these terms and likely have some familiarity with them. We'll teach you more. We suspect you're reading this book because you and someone you care about are unhappy. You've ignored danger signs for too long and now the spark has become a fire and the flames are hot. I'm glad you're here.

The Need for Disruption

Being here and reading this material, as good as it is, is not enough though. You're ready for improvement, you must embrace change. Change requires disruption. Any time we change directions in our life it's because something isn't working. Our inner resistance to change becomes less than our desire to be different, or some force/person, external to us, has created a need for change.

You didn't pick up this book because your life was working but probably quite the opposite. It's not working. You're unhappy. Your mate is unhappy. In all likelihood, your children are unhappy as well. You can no longer tune out the criticism.

However, beyond reading this book, you likely have mixed motives, mixed feelings, and mixed thoughts. You want to change and grow on the one hand but have also found ways to be comfortable with the life you have on the other. You desperately be different.

In the face of mixed feelings and mixed motives, it becomes difficult to chart a new course. Changing directions, after all, requires clarity---and you don't have that.

Danger Signs

Inviting change and embracing disruption requires clarity, which you don't have. Part of the reason you don't have clarity is because you've been ignoring danger signs. We've all ignored danger signs to our own detriment. We've looked at the warning signals on the dash of our car and hoped they would disappear. We've looked at our increased weight, perhaps increased blood pressure, and wished those danger signs didn't exist.

When it comes to issues pertaining to narcissism and emotional abuse, countless men have tried to silence the outer challenges of their mate and the inner convictions of their conscience by saying:

"It can't all be me." (blame shifting)

"Do I really need to change?" (denial)

"Maybe she'll back down." (magical thinking)

"Is she really right?" (minimization)

The questions go on and on and your inner tug-of-war grows in intensity. The struggle intensifies between a desire to be different and the fight to keep life the same.

You've picked up this book because you're losing your inner battle and it's time for a shift of attitude. A complete turnaround. Anything short of that is going to fail.

Making the decision to change, to grow beyond narcissism and emotional abuse requires a change of mind and heart. Many men enter treatment with a profound need to change their minds. Coming to me angry, very frustrated and often feeling like a victim, they've tried fighting back, shifting the focus, deflecting topics, and using many other manipulative tactics, and without exception, they've all failed. The more you fight back, the more you make matters worse.

Shifting Your Focus

In spite of matters growing worse, it is not unusual to tell ourselves that 'things are fine.' This is a rationalization to avoid facing issues. We all attempt to make sense of our lives, and we do so by twisting and distorting the truth.

An example of this twisting of information involves what many men tell me when they begin treatment, or MRC's, The Core Men's Group.

"Dr. Hawkins. I'm a fixer. I want to solve this problem. If she would just tell me what to do, I'd do it. I'm a practical man and I solve problems every day. If she would be clearer with me, I would make any changes she wants."

"You're not the 'fixer' you say you are," I say. "It's a story you've told yourself again and again, but it's not true. If it were true, you would face problems, and we wouldn't be sitting here now. You would lean into the problems that must be faced. You wouldn't make excuses, blame her, play the victim, or feel sorry for yourself."

That usually causes a stir, because we are often deeply attached to the stories, we tell ourselves. But this is at the heart of what we all need to do; challenge our stories and recognize our inner battle between facing issues and ignoring them.

Consider this: Actually, fixing a problem takes a shift in focus and a radical change of perspective. Fixing a problem requires an honest assessment of that problem and then a clear game plan for solving it. Are you ready to do that?

Self-Deception

The stories we tell ourselves, over and over, are interwoven segments of truth and deception. We twist matters to fit the image we have of ourselves, usually distorted to create a favorable self-image.

Many delude themselves with the fantasy that they're facing issues head-on when that is simply not the case. Men come to us believing the following lies:

"I'm really trying."

"I'm doing all I can to solve these problems."

"It's not all my fault."

"I can't work any harder than I am now."

"But it's a two-way street."

"She has to work just as hard as I am."

Have you had any of these thoughts? Any one of these beliefs will keep you stuck. They are all ways of comforting yourself, so you don't feel inner anxiety. Yet, inner anxiety and discomfort are what is needed to shake things up.

These thoughts may temporarily soothe your troubled feelings, but they won't help you move forward. You are deceiving yourself and unless you face this fact, you will never get anywhere. Remember, where you are requires disruption of the stories you are telling yourself.

Lost, One Step at a Time

No one sets out to be lost. We start with good intentions, but we easily become lost, one step at a time.

Airline pilots and navigators know the critical importance of staying on course. Remember that even being as little as one degree off course means winding up one mile off course sixty miles later.

This concept helps us understand how we can be well-intentioned, yet hopelessly lost. A small loss of direction can lead you to be hopelessly lost.

Therefore, course corrections need to be part of our daily life. We all must assume we are heading in the wrong direction, so we are open to correcting our course. Successful people make a habit of constant course correction.

Can you see how you have veered off course? Men, serious about change, must recognize they might be way off course. Tempted to minimize the severity of their situation, they are prone to minimize concerns. Again, we are deceived by the stories we tell ourselves.

Course correction further requires that you set things straight. Any energy you spend focusing on anything other than YOU is wasted. Completed wasted. Any energy you spend not staring at anything other than your problems is wasted. All wasted energy.

So, will you use your energy to get yourself back on the right track, or will you continue to veer off course? Will you focus on your mate, or will you maintain focus on the one person you can actually change—yourself?

Enabling Versus Intervention

Changing course requires disrupting your life---in other words, embracing an intervention. You must course-correct, stepping back and admitting there is a huge problem and you're the only one who can fix it.

We all need to step back, evaluate, and determine if we are expending energy to make necessary changes or using our energies to maintain a certain course.

Enabling is anything you do that maintains the direction you're heading. These may be very subtle decisions. It's important for you to reflect upon all the decisions and actions you regularly take that maintain life exactly as it is.

Any time you focus on others rather than yourself you're enabling a destructive process. You are enabling your current life every time you minimize the harmful effects of your actions. You are enabling every time you distract yourself from the process of change.

Intervention, on the other hand, involves insisting on change. An intervention involves disrupting the status quo. An intervention involves putting your energies into changing direction.

Before changing directions, you need to acknowledge that you've been heading in the wrong direction and make the decision to head in a new direction. You may not be ready for a radical change so interim steps may be helpful, such as reading good literature, attending church, or therapy. These are ways to begin the process of intervention in your life direction.

Another aspect of intervention involves a shift in focus, away from selfish pursuits and onto others in your world— especially your mate. You must shift your focus to the truth of her concerns, your reactions to her concerns, ways to respond to her concerns, and ways to deal with the deeper truths of the issue. First, however, let's look into the life of a man who needs to change.

Jake and the 2-Way Street

Jake is typical of the men who come to the Marriage

Recovery Center. Middle-aged and satisfied in most areas of his life. It has been easy for him to ignore the danger signs of her growing unhappiness and increased complaints.

Sure, his wife had pulled away from him physically, but he rationalized that this was something hormonal with her. She had voiced complaints about him for several years, but he had skillfully shifted the blame back to her.

Her complaints, however, far from lessening, had grown louder. Now she's threatening separation and while he had previously disregarded her concerns, he could no longer ignore them.

Resentful, angry, and feeling cornered, Jake had a bad attitude. He arrived defensive, irritated, and ready to talk about everything but himself.

I braced myself for what I've experienced so many times— a man who uses his energies in all the wrong ways, digging a hole deeper and deeper---enabling a destructive course. I readied myself for a man unlikely to face his issues, refusing an intervention.

"How can I help?" I asked at our initial meeting.

Jake was somber, appearing depressed and irritable.

"My wife says I have to get counseling, or she is going to leave me," he said.

"Okay," I said. "What has led up to this, Jake?"

"She's making mountains out of molehills," he said. "My pastor says the same thing. He knows both of us and can't understand why it has reached this point."

"She must have a reason for making such a threat," I said.

"Look," he said sharply, "I know I'm not perfect, but she has no reason to ask me to leave. I'm not leaving my wife and kids."

Jake went on to share that his wife's threat was incredibly irritating.

"Think about it like this, Jake," I said. "Even if I supported you, even if I believed everything you told me and sided with you, where would that leave you? I would be enabling you to stay the same, and that won't help you. Why don't we dig deeper into this and learn what has gotten her so upset."

"I don't think you've got the full picture," he said. "She moved into a separate bedroom. She's threatening to kick me out if I don't get help from you, experts in narcissism and emotional abuse."

"I'd like to hear more about her complaints," I said.

"She says I'm dismissive and arrogant," he said.

Jake paused.

"I don't think I'm any different from my friends," he said.

"Probably no different than you. I think my wife is trying to blame me. If that's what she needs to do to look herself in the mirror, so be it."

"Is there any truth in what she says?" I asked.

"She says I'm controlling. She says I demand my way. I just don't see it."

"Are these complaints new?" I asked, hoping to create a crack in his defensive armor.

"Not hardly," he answered sarcastically. "She's dragged me to counselor after counselor, for a long time, and I go. She is usually the one to stop going because she doesn't get her way.

Who's the controlling one?"

"It may be that she is screaming to be heard, Jake," I said. "You're not a bad man, but if even some of what she complains about is true, if there is anything to her complaint that you can be arrogant, selfish, and controlling, why not work on that?"

Railing Against Feedback

Jake is typical of other men in our program— defensive, resistive, and not forthcoming. He sees everything his wife does as wrong but sees none of his character weaknesses. He tried to convince me that his wife was wrong. He protested, squirmed, and wiggled to dismiss information he didn't like. His inner struggle was palpable.

We've all been where Jake is. We've all heard information that went against how we see ourselves. We've all gotten a bad report card and wondered how it could possibly happen. It is at these moments that we have a decision to make: do we dismiss the feedback, or do we embrace it? Do we lean into the information, being curious about why someone might be critical of us, or do we fight it?

Many men seeking help from The Marriage Recovery Center enter treatment rigidly, narrow-minded, and argumentative. It is no wonder their wives insist they see "experts" for treatment. These men are typically challenging, and in some instances, nearly impossible to work with.

This can be confusing to those who don't understand emotional abuse because on the surface these men can appear charming. They know when and where to show their aggression, often striving to make a positive impression. They may be leaders in their communities and churches. The perception of these men being selfish and narcissistic clashes with how these men behave in other areas of their lives. But then I remember what Lundy Bancroft, an expert in the field of narcissism and emotional abuse, said.

"The abuser," Bancroft says, "can have significant relationships in his life in which he isn't abusive—as long as it's not his partner relationship or child in the home. His connection to siblings, close friends, employers, or employees, can be pretty normal. That's part of the hell for the abused woman."

Ah, so there it is. While none of what his mate says fits his view of himself, he can be one person to everyone else, and quite another to her.

But how is he able to maintain such contradicting points of view? One word—denial. How are you able to maintain the belief that it's not you she is talking about? Denial! You've decided it's her and so you twist and distort information to fit your story. Something is bugging her, and she's put the blame on you. You're able to come up with twenty explanations for why she's unhappy with you---none of them having to do with legitimate concerns.

Still, her frustrations have grown more intense. The more you fight her, the more depressed she gets. The more you try to get her to back down, the more she backs away. You can't seem to make matters better, and again wonder why you both see things so differently.

While you can continue to fight her allegations, you cannot fight the fact that your marriage is faltering. Sputtering really. There's no getting around the fact that she is miserable with you.

Furthermore, her accusations are sticking to you. They are festering. You've tried not to let them get to you but without luck.

They DO get to you, and you don't like it.

Now there is really only one path forward. You must go on a deep journey, well beyond her accusations and your angry response. You must focus on the truth of her concerns, your reactions to her concerns, ways to respond to her concerns, and ways to deal with the deeper truths of the issue.

Doubt Yourself

It's easy to take Jake's side. He can tell a convincing story of how he's been wronged. Some of it may even be true. If we don't align with him, we might still be tempted to remain neutral. After all, 'it takes two to tango' doesn't it?

Well, not always.

His story requires the listener to dig deeper into his situation. Any listener needs to evaluate how he is talking about his situation. Does he own up to his specific contributions to his marriage issues just as quickly as he points out his wife's actions?

Regardless of who is at fault for what, Jake must face the fact that his wife is ready for a separation if he doesn't more fully accept his part in their problems. It's not a two-way street, at least not now. It's a one-way street, and he better recognize that sooner rather than later.

For Jake to hold fast to his point of view, or for you to do the same, is a certain dead-end. Think about it. While many of us can sit back smugly and cling to our beliefs, to do so leads only to one place---being alone. A wise person once said, "You can be right or be in a relationship, not both. Choose wisely."

So, what is the path forward? The path out of any relational mess is a path of doubting yourself. Oh, I know that the world sells self-confidence, a "you can do it" mentality, but all that bravado has its limits. A surer path involves exploring who you are in contrast to her complaints.

So, let's take another look at Jake. Let's examine his approach. He is strong-minded, sure of himself, and quite intense.

He wants to have control of his life.

But let's read between the lines. Can you imagine trying to counsel him? Sure, mindedness can easily blur into resistance. Firmness can slip into rigidity. Clarity can lead to narrow thinking. Can you see where Jake could become lost in his own point of view?

Imagine being married to Jake. In just a few minutes of sitting with him, I sensed his dominance, his forcefulness. I couldn't help wondering how his wife felt when she tried telling him something he didn't want to hear.

No doubt I was seeing the situation long after the problem began, but could it be that his wife began by asking him to be careful about being dismissive? Is it possible that she has felt unheard, dismissed, perhaps even invisible for a long time? Did she really start out insisting he see "a narcissist expert?" Not likely.

Jake wanted everything to be a "two-way street." Jake wanted to focus on his concerns, not his wife's. Jake is wrong. His insistence on matters being a "two-way street" led only to him being stuck. His focusing on his wife's issues led only to him not focusing on his own.

Why do I say Jake is wrong? Because, at this point, it's not a two-way street. Remember, it can become a two-way street in time, but not now. Now, it's a one-way street—it's about Jake opening his mind, letting go of his pride, and exploring why his wife is adamant about him needing to change.

More Self-Doubt

Self-doubt means opening your mind and being teachable. Self-doubt can be such a healthy perspective because it creates a window to our inner world, where self-confidence cheats us.

There is a tool we use with men that will become invaluable to you as you begin this book: first thought wrong. What do I mean by 'first thought wrong?' I mean you must step back and reconsider everything you think. It means not only must you step back to reevaluate, but you must doubt much of what you believe. I want you to assume that your thinking is off.

After all, if you don't need to check your attitude if you don't need to 'course correct,' why are you here? It's because your first thought may very well be wrong, and you need to be open to new information. Learning only takes place when we take the role of a student. We must cultivate an openness every time we want to learn something new. This shouldn't be too surprising to hear since learning occurs with an open and receptive attitude.

Dr. Hudson and I have found that most men struggling with narcissistic tendencies struggle with close-mindedness. Their certainty has become rigidity. Their sureness has become denial and self-centeredness. If you are going to learn from your mate and understand why she has used the 'narcissist' label, you must be willing to consider points of view that might be offensive to you. You must consider 'first thought wrong' and doubt yourself, recognizing you need a coach. Openness and receptivity lead to growth and the possibility of change.

Embracing Her Concerns

Jake's resistance and argumentativeness are not unusual, and it certainly doesn't mean he can't be helped. With backs against the wall and feeling threatened, many men become oppositional. They rigidly attach to old ways of viewing themselves. Instead of embracing self-doubt, and "first thought wrong," they hold to their outdated and distorted self-concept--- not a recipe for change.

What is the recipe for change? We recommend taking a critical look at her accusations, sitting with them, and actually embracing them. You must thoroughly explore the accusations and concerns she has brought to you. The only way around the thorny question of narcissism is through it.

The only reasonable path forward is a radically different approach. This will take some getting used to. Giving up ground won't come easily. We recommend the following steps:

Stop protesting, defending, arguing. This isn't rocket science. What do you gain by fighting, arguing, counterattacking? Nothing. You only make matters worse. When you argue, defend, and protest, you actually add fuel to her fire. You essentially 'make her case.'

Consider her concerns. Why has she called you a narcissist? The label is simply a shortened way of explaining a more complex idea. What does she mean? What are her concerns? She deserves to be heard and fully understood, right? So, find out what she means.

Is she really saying that you're selfish? Is she saying you're bullheaded? Is she saying you are domineering and controlling? Is she saying you are insensitive? This is a time to question yourself and ask more questions of her.

Remind yourself that she's trying to get your attention. Why? Because she wants a relationship with you. If she didn't care about you and the marriage she would simply walk away. She is trying to get your attention. She's not calling names to simply insult you. No, she wants your attention and is likely desperately seeking change.

Let's get something straight. You can silence your mate with defensiveness—for sure. You can blame shift, deny, stonewall, pout, erupt in anger, minimize your actions, all in an effort to silence her, but the problem will not, absolutely will not, go away. Calling you a narcissist is simply her way of describing an attitude or behavior that needs attention.

Embrace and lean into her concerns. Since you can't MAKE the problem go away, why not lean into it? Since denial, dismissal, and domination only make matters far worse, why not do the brave thing and lean in? Face the music. Sit with your discomfort and embrace her criticisms and concerns.

Whether you are or are not a narcissist is another matter. What is likely true is that you have some traits that are concerning enough to make her call you one. So, step up, lean in, and embrace her concerns. Tell her you are ready to get down to business. Enough avoidance. Enough defensiveness. It's time to 'man up' and listen to her.

Finally, do the work. Ah, now we get to the subtitle of this book: doing the work to end narcissism and emotional abuse.

Someone smarter than me said this: naming the problem is half the problem solved. So true. Once we name an issue, we can get on with the task of solving the issue. All energy used to deny the problem is not only wasted energy but makes matters worse, prolonging the problem.

Ten Simple Questions

I hope you are beginning to self-reflect and embrace her concerns. We want to help you get unstuck, get beyond any labels, and embrace specific concerns. We want you to let go of pride and defensiveness and get on with the spirit of collaboration—working together to solve a problem.

If you're still struggling, here are a few questions to consider. Please answer 'true or false' to each question as your mate would likely answer them. Bear in mind, each of these items is a starting place for even more robust conversations.

My opinions, feelings, and choices are not respected or heard.

I do not feel safe in bringing concerns to you. When I do, I am met with either aggression or stonewalling.

I can never talk about issues without you becoming extremely defensive and angry. I am rarely able to resolve issues.

I feel discouraged, worthless, voiceless, and invisible in the relationship.

I sense that you care very little about my likes, dislikes, values, hopes, and desires.

I feel like I am always walking on eggshells.

I often feel anxious when around you.

I have little desire to celebrate and enjoy you.

I feel chronic stress, fatigue, insomnia, and pain.

Because of my overall unhappiness, I have strongly considered leaving the relationship.

What did you discover? Did you notice some trends and patterns? We want you to discover patterns, and themes in your relationships. You see, any concern that your mate has raised has, in all likelihood, been raised many times before. Pay attention.

Stumbling Blocks to an Open Mind

Another potential stumbling block to listening with an open mind concerns the issue of overt abuse versus covert abuse--- overt abuse is actions seen by anyone when they occur. The actions of covert abuse are more subtle, often going unnoticed by anyone other than the victim.

An example of overt abuse would be when a man reacts angrily, vents profanity, and walks out of the room. That same man may also abuse covertly, or passively, by withdrawing into silence and pouting when things don't go the way he wants.

Most men deny any overt abuse, and therefore can't understand how they might be labeled abusive. They justify their actions by thinking, "I have never hit her," or "I have never screamed at her." Yet, they are abusive.

It is critical to fully understand the distinction between overt and covert narcissism. Overt narcissists stand out! We see their flamboyant or aggressive antics. They are typically loud, obnoxious, antagonistic, and aggressive. We SEE their actions. We

HEAR their voice. We can all point to that individual and say, "There goes a narcissist!"

But make no mistake, covert actions, repeated again and again, are very damaging and take a tremendous toll.

Harm in the Shadows

It's important for you to see, and acknowledge, the harm that is done quietly and in the shadows of daily life. Much emotional abuse takes place where others cannot see it, or if they see the bad behavior, many are reluctant to label it abuse.

Imagine having a broken arm. Now imagine that your family ignores your requests to be careful around you and your broken arm. They bump into it again and again, each time saying they are sorry.

Soon you become irritable. You accuse them of being insensitive, while they complain that you are being too sensitive. They bump into your arm again and again, aggravating not only your arm but your mood as well. A small matter quickly becomes larger and more significant.

Let's bring the matter closer to home. Take the example of the man who withdraws into silence when offended. He doesn't do that with his friends, of course, but he does it with his wife. What is the impact on his wife who feels his distance time and again?

Most don't consider this abuse, but it is. Any harmful pattern inflicted again and again has the possibility of being abusive. In fact, emotional abuse has been called 'the silent epidemic' because neither victim nor perpetrator talk openly about it.

In all likelihood, you have spent years trying to convince her that your actions were not so bad. You have spent years invalidating her experience, creating confusion in her mind. So, can you really blame her for not speaking out?

Remember she still loves you. She desperately wants to make the marriage work. She wants to believe you. You're not all bad and she knows that. So, she is very confused and is probably asking herself some of the same questions you're asking yourself.

So, we must all join forces to bring the emotional abuse out of the shadows and into the light where we can talk openly about them and make good decisions about how to move forward. That will be the only way to save the relationship.

Owning and ending harm is certainly a major part of what must occur. However, even more is needed to make progress. Real progress involves letting go of your old mindset, which was filled with denial and blaming others, and taking full responsibility for healing. This is a recovery mindset.

A Recovery Mindset

A powerful way to begin making changes is to step back, take a new direction, and embrace a recovery mindset. Did you know that there is a recovery mindset? It's true. People who embrace recovery have a different mindset toward recovery than those who do not. I'll explain.

It is well-known that a person's mindset sets the stage for their recovery, whether we are talking about an upcoming surgery, a dental procedure, recovery from an addiction, or, in this instance, recovery from being a perpetrator of emotional abuse.

Take these real examples:

Paul entered treatment for emotional abuse telling me everything was his wife's fault. He accused her of exaggerating his actions, just like Jake. He was angry, easily ruffled, dismissive, and questioned why he was even in our Core Men's Group.

"I'll make no bones about it. I'm here because she's holding our marriage over my head. She said she would leave me if I didn't do the group, so I'm here."

"What do you hope to get out of the group?" I asked.

"I don't have any hopes for the group," he said. "I'm doing it to get her off my back."

There was silence in the group.

"Paul," I said, "if you can't find a better reason for being here, you're not likely to get much from this experience. I encourage you to think about her concerns and what you might have to learn."

"He's voicing some of my same feelings," Stan said. "I don't really feel like I'm free to choose the group or not." Another man, Jeffrey, spoke next.

"I've been where Paul's at," Jeffrey began. "I'm not saying I'm any better than he is. My wife also said I had to join this group, but I've thought about why she is insistent about it, and I've decided she has good reason. I've been impossible to live with my wife insisting I come to this group, is just the latest in her efforts to get me to see how difficult I've been. I've created this situation and now it's time for me to step up and face the issues."

"Your attitude is refreshing, Jeffrey," I said. "You're absolutely right about your wife. Women don't insist on change because they want to be controlling. They have been asking for change for a long time and most of you haven't been listening. This group is an opportunity to really listen."

I paused, looking at the other men in the group.

"You all have a decision to make," I continued. "Do you cop an attitude, fighting your mate all the way? If you do, you squander an opportunity and make matters far worse. Or do you embrace her concerns?"

I sat quietly with the men as they considered my words.

Imagine being Paul's wife. She has asked him, again and again, to get help. Because he has been abusive, she has begged him to get professional help. Because of becoming easily annoyed and resistant, he's not only resisted counseling but has blamed shifted all their problems onto her. He has insisted that everyone else needs to change!

Now, imagine this goes on day after day, month after month, year after year. I can assure you that this kind of dominance would wear anyone down. This rigidity, this lack of resilience and cooperation, this stubbornness, IS emotionally abusive.

Changing Your Mind/ Changing Your Heart

It is one thing to decide to be different, which every man in the group says they want to do. However, the ones who succeed in changing make a heartfelt commitment to change. They have a change of heart as well as a change of mind. This will not be easy. You will need to critically examine who you are and what you believe. You will need to fully dive into examining your heart.

Scripture says, "For the mouth speaks what the heart is full of. A good man brings good things out of the good things stored up in him, and an evil man brings evil things out of the evil stored up in him." (Matthew 12: 34-40)

Now, there is nothing revolutionary about this. Consider again Paul, Stan, and Jeffrey. All three spoke what was stored up in their hearts. Everything that spilled out in the group had undoubtedly been previously heard by their mates.

This is such a critical concept: We broadcast our very integrity, our personhood, to everyone, all the time. We might keep our mouths shut sometimes, but again, "the mouth speaks what the heart is full of," and so we can discern a lot about a person by the attitudes they convey.

Can I say for sure that Paul is emotionally abusive? No.

But has he broadcast the kind of person he is? Has he revealed to us what is in his heart? Yes. Does his wife feel his resentment? For sure.

This is part of the reason we promote 'depth counseling' to men. We don't want superficial change. We want to hold up a giant mirror and invite men to explore what is hidden in their hearts.

Thankfully, each of these men's attitudes and actions can be changed. Men who want to change, can. Men who recognize and own their dismissive, defensive, and dominant attitudes can, with focus and clear intentions, change and grow. But this takes deliberate effort.

A Decision to Embrace Growth

Every day we face and make multiple decisions. Will we get up a bit earlier to work out or will we sleep in? Will we choose healthy options for lunch, or do we go for a quick and less healthy meal? Will we spend any time in prayer and reflection, or will we scurry through the day?

Every decision brings certain consequences. Every decision propels our life in a particular direction. Your life, however, it is going, is exactly the way you've designed it to be.

So, think about it. Take a moment and reflect upon where you live, how you live, and with whom you live. Each is the result of choices made earlier in your life. Your life situation is largely the result of choices you have made, some good and others perhaps not so good.

In the same way, today you face the opportunity to embrace change and growth. Like Paul, you have the choice to blame others for your situation and remain an angry victim. You can rehearse that you've gotten a bad rap, that you're suffering from unfortunate circumstances. Your choices will then be very limited.

Or, like Jeffrey, you can understand and accept that you are exactly where you've chosen to be and can now make better, healthier choices. Today can be a new beginning.

So, with that goal in mind, let's get on with it. Every chapter is designed to challenge you, question you, enlighten you, and give you a new path forward.

Embracing Change
Chapter Two: Dr. David B. Hawkins

You've been confronted with labels of narcissism and emotional abuse. This has caused you to take a step back and learn about some of the traits of narcissism and covert and overt abuse. This has led you to take time to reflect and consider the possibility of letting go of some old patterns of relating. Knowing you must change, if you've decided to change, keep reading.

Change is easier said than done. It means giving up a way of life that means something to you. This is why changing is so incredibly difficult. It's why most people underestimate the challenge of changing as well as what is required of those who embrace change.

Change is difficult and is a big undertaking. People talk positively about the changes they expect to make, only to have most plans end in failure. Many talk about change, yet few set themselves up to embrace it.

You have undoubtedly come to this chapter somewhat aware that change is needed in your life, but that's where things break down. You must have a clear understanding of the changes that need to be made. Knowing you need to change is not enough. You must embrace change.

For as much as you want to change, your habits and life patterns need to be disrupted. Being serious about changing involves reorienting your life to accommodate new ways of thinking and behaving, and this is often a challenge. Again, you must embrace change.

What Do You Need to Change?

Before you can make changes in your life, you must identify what it is you're attempting to change. Simple, right? Not at all. I'll give you a recent example from my own life.

I teach vulnerability and sensitivity yet have failed at times to truly practice it in my own life. I pride myself in being a good man,' yet my wife, Christie, recently challenged me—again.

"David," she began after asking me to sit down, "I'm feeling alone again. You've gotten busy with your own things—piano, Spanish, tennis, writing---all good things. But they don't include me."

"Wow," I responded defensively. "I've asked you about all those things."

"Yes, but you haven't kept up with my feelings. I want to be a bigger part of your life. I want to be included. I don't want to live alone."

I had to quiet my defenses to really hear her. I had to be willing to review all those activities—all good things—in ways to make sure I was including her. After a few speed bumps that included feeling inadequate, I'm excited at the new level of connection we are feeling.

In order to make changes I had to be honest with myself about the ways I included, and didn't include, my wife. I had to honestly evaluate what needed to change. This was not easy work but was worthwhile work.

What did I learn from this experience? I learned that I need to review what I'm trying to accomplish and the best methods for accomplishing my goals. I learned that I need to be critical, focused, and wise in my choices. I need to know what exactly I want to change and the best methods for changing.

The same is true for you.

Have you determined what exactly you want to change? Do you want to change patterns of emotional abuse? Why? You must learn how you are going to make those changes. In Chapter One you learned about taking a step back and critically reviewing your life. You must have a clear and effective plan. Your specific plan must create a real opportunity for making those changes.

The process of embracing change is complicated but begins with a certain attitude that we call a 'Change Mindset.'

Embracing A Change Mindset

Change is difficult because successful change involves disrupting current routines and establishing new routines. Becoming aware of your routines is critical to setting change in motion. Embracing a 'change mindset' means becoming comfortable, at least for a time, with disrupting routines.

We all have routines. Our brain actually loves habits because then we don't have to think. We can slide lazily from one habit to another.

We've worked long and hard to establish routines and habits and don't give them up easily.

What will I have for breakfast tomorrow? Yogurt and granola. And what about the next day? Probably yogurt and granola again. And what brand? My favorite brand with the bear on the cover. Why will I have granola and yogurt again and again? Because I like it, and it has become a habit.

When will I go to bed? About ten o'clock. Why? You guessed it. It's another habit. Not a bad thing. Habits give my life meaning. I'm a granola and yogurt lover, as well as a '10 o'clock bedtime goer.' That's me and that's the good news. Now how about the bad news?

Habits can also keep us stuck—stuck in predictable ways of acting and thinking, inflexible and guarded about needed change. Habits, if not critically reviewed, keep us stuck in patterns established long ago. Remember, our brains love habits because we don't have to think. Our brain knows exactly what to do and how to move without effort from one situation to the next.

This is also called inertia. Isaac Newton discovered that 'a body in motion stays in motion, and a body at rest stays at rest.' We all experience it. This law is the reason some people can more effectively 'stay in motion' and others 'stay at rest.' It's all about the habits we've created and reinforced, again and again.

I hadn't considered doing anything different about my weekly routines until it was too late. The damage of distance in my marriage had grown, step by step, outside of my awareness. I had become lazy; my brain liked my habits and change was now more difficult.

Since a body at rest stays at rest, it takes more energy to change patterns, to create new habits. It will be critical to understand and appreciate this principle as you move ahead, making changes in your life. Changing requires energy and serious intention.

So, do you want to change? I mean, really? If so, you need to disrupt your life. You need to prepare for change and prepare for inner resistance to change. Remember, your brain is satisfied with the status quo and so you must uncover and create compelling reasons to change.

Stirring Up Motivation

Your status quo needs attention, and so you need to summon some very strong motivation in order to change.

Remember, part of you is perfectly satisfied with the status quo, so why change? Reflect on what you want to change and why you want to change. Your motivation to change must be strong because it is the fuel for the energy you'll need to make changes.

Your narcissistic patterns are entrenched. You've had them, and reinforced them, for a long time. You need to want to change if you are to overcome natural resistance. Have you summoned the intensity required to dismantle old patterns? Do you have an inner determination to not settle for your old ways of doing things? If not, you cannot expect to change.

Your life is in turmoil. It's time to use that turmoil as fuel for change. After all, dissatisfaction creates motivation for change.

My desire to recreate a connection to my wife comes from unrest and tension, and that unrest creates motivation to change. Dissatisfaction with the way our life currently is creates the impetus to change. So again, consider what exactly you want to change and why you want to change. Sit with it. Embrace it.

That brings us closer to the reason for writing, and your reason for reading this book---eliminating chronic, pervasive patterns of emotional abuse. Your desire and need for change have grown out of the immense harm you have done. Someone, presumably a partner, has said they will no longer stay connected to you if you don't change.

Think about this. Think about her. Picture your current situation, and the harm you have done again and again, and then remind yourself why you need to make changes.

If this is not enough motivation to change, evaluate who you are in contrast to who you ideally want to be. Do you want to be a more caring person? This could provide good impetus for change. Do you want to be a person who doesn't harm another person? This, too, could be a strong impetus for change.

Being clear and choosing to make changes in yourself is the first step, but again, change does not come easily. There will be barriers that may stop you from changing. Let's consider some of those.

Barriers to Change

As we learned earlier, disrupting the status quo isn't easy, but it is critical. You must understand your brain has established many patterns for maintaining life just the way it is. These may be stronger than your desire to change. Do you recognize that?

At this moment, more of you may want this problem to just go away rather than read this book or engage in counseling. Be honest with yourself about this. Let's explore some of the barriers to change. These must be recognized and addressed.

Mixed Motives

We all have mixed motives---pros and cons to anything we do. We want to undertake something new in our lives and we don't want to undertake something new. We must become aware of those 'pros and cons,' those 'mixed motives' so we are clear about our choices.

Sure, you affirm that it would be good to be different. Okay, but unless you fully commit, unless you clearly dedicate your actions fully, change won't happen. Change is simply too challenging an undertaking to be done half-heartedly.

The Alcoholics Anonymous program is famous for teaching "half measures avail us nothing." Having worked with hundreds of men, and their mates, I can tell you it's true. She is sick and tired of trying to get you to change, hearing excuse after excuse. She is tired of your mixed motives.

She is exhausted from trying to get you to read books, watch videos, and attend counseling.

For every concern she raised, you raise counter-arguments:

"No one else says I need to change."

"She needs to change just as much as I do."

"These aren't big issues, just small personality differences."

"I've been working on it."

And so, it goes. Half-hearted efforts with very mixed motives. You want to change, and you don't want to change, and those forces often cancel one another out. You need to resolve this in your mind.

My mixed motives were confronted by my wife. It was my job to resolve that imbalance in my mind. For as much as I wanted to cling to my old way of doing things, I wanted to connect with her more. Mixed motives would not work.

This matter wasn't settled in an instant. She'd brought up this issue in the past, and I had settled back into my old ways. I wanted to change, and I didn't want to change.

"I do care about your life," I said. What I didn't voice, which was also true, was "I don't want to change. I like my habits." Mixed motives.

"No, you fit me into the spaces of your life," she continued. "Your life is filled with you, your interests. I need you to take an active interest in me."

I considered her words and fought an inner battle. I wanted to feel normal, balanced, and self-protected, but to change I needed to feel uneasy, unsettled, and ruffled, for this unrest to lead to change. Mixed motives would lead to----nothing.

I want to be a good husband. More importantly, I want to feel connected to my wife and want her to feel connected to me. This is very important to me and it's important to my wife. Win, win. Half-measures, and mixed motives, won't get me to where I want to go.

Trying Versus Training

Craig Groeschel, Senior Pastor of Life Church in Oklahoma, and author of the book, When Trying Alone Won't Change Your Life, reveals another barrier to change.

"Trying", he shares, whether about losing weight, being a healthier human, or perhaps in issues pertaining to emotional abuse, is about having a vague goal, with a limited commitment and no accountability. "Trying" is about having a limited vision typically with very limited results.

"Training," however, he asserts, is something very different. The person in training has very clear and specific goals, a dedicated commitment, and habits around that commitment that make success likely.

We don't need to feel bad about our ambivalence but rather face our true reality. It's not our ambivalence that thwarts our efforts, but our lack of honesty, and the subsequent courage to make hard decisions based upon the truth.

As I watch superstar tennis players like Rafael Nadal, Roger Federer, or Novak Djokovic, I remind myself that they have spent countless hours training to become the stars they are. They have dedicated themselves to perfecting their craft. If I want to be successful in changing, I need to be training rather than simply trying, and so do you.

Magical Thinking/ Denial

Another barrier to change is magical thinking. Magical thinking is one aspect of D.E.N.I.A.L--Don't Even Notice I Am Lying to Myself.

Magical thinking is minimizing our wrongdoing, making our problems out to be far less onerous than they are. It involves making excuses for our actions, distracting ourselves from the severity of our situation, blaming others for our problems, or justifying our actions.

Magical thinking sounds like:

"Everything will work out" (without clear plans and goals)

"I'm doing the best I can" (when that is not true)

"I'm working on it" (with no clear timeline)

Magical thinking is just that—magical, like waving a magic wand and expecting positive results. Life does not work that way. We eliminate magical thinking when we squarely face our problems and seek reasonable remedies for them.

Stages of Change

It's time to get real and be honest. It's time for you to step back and assess how serious you are about changing. You may not be as far along as you imagine.

Prochaska and DiClemente, authors of a famous theory on change, suggest there are five stages of change. These five stages are recognized as the process by which we move from considering a problem to fully embracing it. Where are you in regard to issues pertaining to narcissism and emotional abuse?

Precontemplation: You have not yet acknowledged that there is a problem that needs to be changed.

Contemplation: You have acknowledged that there is a problem but are not yet ready, sure of wanting, or lack the confidence to make a change.

Preparation/ Determination: You are getting ready to make changes. You have made a commitment to change and are researching possible change paths.

Action/ Willpower: You are motivated to make changes to your behavior and are actively involved in taking steps to change bad behavior.

Maintenance: Not only do you move forward with change, but now, most importantly, you avoid any temptations to return to the bad behavior that led to change. The goal of the maintenance stage is to maintain the new status quo.

These stages of change are similar to the twelve steps of Alcoholics Anonymous, with each step building upon the previous one. If, at any time someone makes a misstep, or relapses, they move back to start again. So, it is with the 5 stages of change.

Why You Might Resist Change

After reading about the stages of change, don't be surprised if you discover you're not as far along as you imagined. Likewise, don't be surprised if you discover more reasons why you have not embraced change.

Let's dive a little deeper. Let's expose some of the underlying reasons why you might not want to change. Remind yourself that ambivalence is normal, but dishonesty (denial) is what will really thwart your efforts.

Why Might You Not Want to Change?

I'm comfortable in my own skin. It's likely that you've been living with your behavior and thought patterns for a long time—a lifetime. You are familiar with them. You know you, and perhaps you mostly like who you are. The degree to which you embrace your thoughts—being comfortable in your skin—will possibly determine how much change you will embrace.

It takes energy, focus, and commitment. We have a natural tendency to simply keep doing what we've always done, in the ways we've always done them. Not a bad thing at all. Just a tendency to conduct our lives the same way every day. Change requires you to marshal your energies, bringing a new sense of focus and commitment to doing things differently.

It will disrupt my life. Change requires that you give up certain habits and patterns of behaving and act in new ways, thereby disrupting the status quo. If you are going to lose weight, you must do many things differently, like more exercise and changing eating habits. Likewise, if you're going to change patterns of emotional abuse, you will need to form new habits, thus disrupting your life. Treatment which will be a necessary part of your new lifestyle, disrupting your life.

It will take reorganizing my life and creating new habits. Treatment and dedication to a change process require reorganizing your life. You need to make room for new reading, new thinking, new journaling, and new relationships. You need to give up the habits that reinforce emotional abuse and embrace new habits that reinforce healthy thinking and relating.

It will take time. Treatment and change take time. Training, after all, cannot be squeezed into the nooks and crannies of life. If you place treatment and your goals for change onto the edge of your plate, they will certainly fall off when the juggling of commitments occurs. You must make sufficient time for your treatment goals.

It will take financial challenges.

Treatment costs money.

Accessing the right and possibly best resources will take a financial commitment. It is generally agreed that we put our financial resources behind things that are important to us, so you must make a decision to spend money on getting healthy.

Resentment and resistance. Treatment involves listening to and following advice. Some men discover a strong resistance to being told what to do or how to do it. You may discover that you don't want to be pushed, you don't want anyone telling you that you must change. Be very careful. Don't resist change simply because you are resisting someone.

Layers of Protection

Change is difficult and you must understand the challenge you are facing. Underestimating the size of the challenge is the number one reason people fail to make the changes they want.

We've explored barriers to reaching our goals, so now let's explore another powerful reason many men fail to make the changes they want: the very behavior you want to change may be a protection or a pattern that has helped you meet needs.

You may tell yourself you really want to change, but is it possible that your old behaviors meet some need for protection, and thus you cling to old patterns out of self-protection? Is it possible that buried within the layers of your mind you have another hidden agenda---protecting yourself with these bad behaviors?

Tom, one man in our Core group, shared the following story:

"I've discovered that I like my angry outbursts. This was really hard to admit. Giving my anger a lot of thought I discovered I feel strong and powerful when I'm angry as opposed to feeling vulnerable when I'm meek and quiet. I guess I never learned how to speak up for myself and my anger is the only way I know to be heard. I'm afraid of feeling weak or being viewed as weak. My dad teased me when I was afraid or "weak" and so I ran from those feelings. I think I'm bringing that baggage into my marriage."

Notice that this man's old behavior was serving a purpose-- protecting him from vulnerable feelings he has had since childhood. This doesn't at all mean it was good for him, or others, but it was serving a purpose and would not be easy to eliminate. Old behaviors often "help" some aspect of ourselves and we must really understand this concept if we are going to make significant changes.

Tom's insights were quite a revelation. Understanding himself, and the layers of protection he had created, gave him the motivation to learn more about his vulnerable self and his need to learn healthy expression. It provided him a window into seeing himself in new ways.

He has used these insights to rethink whether these layers of protection, which were useful at one point in his life, were helping him now. He weighed out the costs of maintaining the protection against the rewards of change, something we all must do.

Is your bad behavior offering protection for you? Do you have unmet needs that are clamoring for attention? There are healthier ways to meet your needs, and these insights can provide you with the motivation you need for change.

Motivation to Change

Your efforts to change must be supported by deeply held, powerful motives. You need energy, focus, and dogged commitment to really change. You must be 'in training' rather than 'trying.' Are you being honest with yourself about that difference?

If you've decided you want to change, you must know exactly why. You're learning about motives that will help you, and others that will fail you. This has to do with internal versus external motives.

Remember Jake? He came into our Core Treatment Group with external motivations.

"I need to change because my wife won't stop complaining," he shared in his first treatment group session. "She is not going to stop nagging me until I do something, so here I am."

"But do you want to change for you?" a group member asked.

"It's not whether I want to change or not," Jake continued.

"She won't stop harping on me until I do."

"We get that," the member added, "but do you think you need to change?"

"Look," he said, obviously getting upset, "whether I want to change or not, I have to do this so I'm here."

"Not a good reason for being here," a second group member added. "Being here for her won't be enough motivation for real change.

I've been there, done that. It doesn't work. You've got to be here for you, for reasons that are important to you."

Jake was agitated by being confronted by men he thought would align with him. The second member had even more to say.

"I'm not trying to get on your case, but you have some thinking to do. I've been where you're at and it just doesn't work. You need to find your reasons for being here. Don't just come because she's threatening you."

This was a critical moment in our group and an opportunity for the men to examine their own motives. The men discussed the topic of 'motivations for change' and came up with the following list:

Our relationship is filled with turmoil and conflict, and we are also unhappy.

We act and think in ways we don't like, and neither does she.

We want to grow emotionally and relationally, and she wants that for me.

We have deeply held spiritual convictions that call for radical change.

We want to be a better person for our mate.

Jake's struggle was very familiar to all the men in the group. They had been, or were still, where he was emotionally. Simply satisfying his wife's insistence on being in a group would not sustain lasting change—only deeply held, internal motivations would do that.

That group ended with a sobering thought issued by one member:

"Think about what will happen if you choose not to change."

What If I Don't Change?

It's not popular to think about what could happen if you don't change, but it is possibly the most potent motivator for change. Considering the repercussions of not changing is an integral aspect of many relapse prevention programs, for good reason.

I've shared this story before, but it bears repeating here. A number of years ago I had several mishaps involving speeding. I took my first speeding citation in stride. It wouldn't happen again, I told myself, but continued driving as I always had, intent on getting to my destination.

Less than a week later I was pulled over again for speeding. This time I was annoyed at the officer for stopping me. It wasn't my fault, I rationalized. For the next several days I groused about the officer 'hiding under an overpass on the freeway.' I had let my focus lapse.

Another week passed and—you guessed it---I was stopped again for speeding. If you're counting, this was three speeding tickets in three weeks.

At this point, I was angry with myself. However, my challenges were only beginning. I received a letter in the mail from the Department of Licensing inviting me to attend a Safe Driving class. The letter added that if I failed to attend and complete the class AND refrain from any citations for six months, my license would be suspended.

This grabbed my attention. I realized that if I didn't change, I wouldn't be driving. I immediately took that letter and taped it to the dash of my car, reminding me what would happen if I failed to change.

Let me assure you this experience taught me some lasting lessons. I learned that the government is serious about enforcing the law. I learned that my actions could lead to serious consequences. I also learned that I needed to give up my immature attitude about speeding and change.

While we're not talking about speeding in this book, we are talking about change—behavior change and letting go of denial. What behavior patterns do you need to change? What heart attitudes need changing? What will happen if you don't change?

A Nice-Guy Narcissist

Not all narcissists and emotional abusers are outrightly aggressive. Some are much more covert in their abuse. Steven was an emotionally abusive man who needed treatment just as much as other men in our Core program. Like others, however, he entered our Core Treatment Group resisting change. His resistance wasn't the aggressive angry type, however, but rather the passive resistive kind.

Steven had been attending couples counseling for some time prior to entering the group, so I knew him. Known as a 'nice guy,' he didn't fit any of the markers we typically think fit a narcissist. In fact, he is seen by most as a jovial, fun-loving person.

As I got to know Steven, however, and after speaking with his wife, I found his behavior was just as destructive as more overtly aggressive men. His wife was exhausted from his verbal commitment to change with no action.

"Is it me?" Theresa asked in a session. "He is nice to everyone, but he drains me. He acts like a little boy. He pouts if he doesn't get his way. He sulks around the house when he's upset. If

I confront him, he withdraws for days. I didn't want another child.

I hate it."

Steven resisted change. While not blatantly resistive, he was passive-resistant, offering superficial ownership for his actions, and vowing to change, but again there was no follow through.

Steven's inaction caused immense harm to his marriage. No one other than his wife would feel his passive-aggressive actions, but over time these character traits caused serious harm.

Sustained Effort

It will not be easy, at least at first, to see the harm Steven perpetrates since it's his inaction causing so much harm. Steven's emotional abuse stems from neglect—profound, repeated neglect.

It may be the same with you. The weight of responsibility is real. Sustained effort, as Steven is learning, is heavy. It's much easier to promise the moon and under-deliver.

Steven is learning the hard way that empty promises create a deeper hole to dig out of. He's learning that inaction is actually action. As one woman said, "You may not be *trying* to harm me, but you're not trying to *not* harm me, and that's just as bad."

This is very true. Emotional neglect, lacking a sustained effort to change, is abusive. Harm occurs from the failure to keep promises, to give to others what you've promised to give them in terms of attention, care, and compassion.

Change happens for the person who is very deliberate about the change they desire. Consider the changes that have been asked of you. You must focus on those changes and be serious and ready to offer sustained effort. Then it's time to set your life up to fully support behavioral and attitudinal changes.

Building Change Habits

Change requires setting clear goals and making many small changes that support that goal. Our habits are connected to each other, forming patterns, all that must be disrupted and reorganized.

Remember my goal of connecting with my wife? It was not enough to simply want to connect—I had to critically review all my destructive habits that led to inattention to her.

When you want to change one habit, many other aspects of your life support that habit. If you don't change all the supporting habits, you will likely regress.

Experts in the field of 'relapse prevention' know the number one reason for relapse is not taking relapse seriously. Said another way, the person who slips back hasn't changed enough of the 'habit patterns' that lead to change.

It is natural to slip back and regress if you haven't altered your life (your habits) in ways to support change.

Remember, one habit often supports another habit. That's the way it works. I'm working at breaking old habits, disrupting the status quo, and creating new healthy habits, such as being present with my wife. As I create new habits, I no longer have to fret or worry about making changes. My brain 'knows' what to do and the changes take care of themselves.

Someone said, "Nothing beats success like success." I want to stay connected to my wife and so have set new goals of inviting her into my life, in large and small ways. I think about reviewing my day with her as well as being mindful of her day. Reviewing and changing all of the habits that played a role in my inattention is critical for real change. I've also noticed that confidence in this one area gives me confidence that I can apply to other tasks and goals.

Preparing For Setbacks and Staying the Course

Not all change is about progress. Change theorists don't hesitate to talk about setbacks. It is normal and natural to regress, and you should expect it. However, setbacks can be minimized, and learning should take place with each setback.

It's important to cultivate a sense of watchfulness about your progress, anticipating where and how setbacks are likely to occur. You must cultivate awareness of where you are regarding your goals so that you are constantly reexamining your goals and your progress toward those goals.

So, again, what are you trying to change? Success comes from being in training, with specific goals and habits that support those changes, as opposed to simply trying, with vague goals. Part of being in training requires you to face and anticipate setbacks.

Setbacks, as challenging as they are, teach us a lot. I challenge you to think about ways you've had setbacks and what you learned from them. Typically, setbacks occur because of one of the following:

1. Failing to fully incorporate the changes into your daily life. Weave the proposed changes into your lifestyle, much the way I have recently with my connection to my wife.
2. Failing to ensure monitoring and feedback regarding your proposed changes. Watch your progress. Journal about your progress. Talk to others about your progress.
3. Failing to watch for regression. Monitor where, when, and how regression occurs and learn from the experience.
4. Failing to notice and embrace positive changes. Take note of the efforts you are putting into change and the impact those changes are having on you and your relationships.
5. Failure to celebrate your successes. Celebrate your success and the good that comes about due to your changes.

If you have experienced setbacks, have you doubled your efforts or have you indulged your disappointments? Indulging your disappointments means wallowing in self-pity, thinking you cannot make progress, or you'll never be good enough. Real progress requires reevaluating goals, perhaps adjusting them, and then staying the course.

Embracing Your Inner Change Cheerleader

To continuously embrace change involves offering yourself encouragement. Remember, change is difficult, and we all need encouragement. Since others won't always be there to support us, we must support ourselves.

Don't be afraid to ask for encouragement and don't forget that it will be easier to offer encouragement to yourself if you set realistic goals. Baby steps! Review your expectations and ensure they are realistic. Share your goals with a trusted friend, therapist, or support group.

Remember, there is no harm in asking others for support and encouragement. Tell friends about the changes you are making. Tell your mate that you would like to receive encouragement for the changes you are making. Don't expect encouragement but ask for it.

Finally, consider being part of a therapy group that promotes change. Sitting with others on a similar journey can feel very encouraging. Having others witness the significant changes you are trying to make can feel good.

Offering encouragement to others as they work at making significant changes can also be an important part of your journey. Let others know the changes you are making and ask to be held accountable for very specific goals.

Finally, it is important to recognize that change is not a linear process. 'Two steps forward, one back' is more often the case. Sometimes it's two steps forward, two back and sometimes it's three steps forward. All in all, you will feel the progress as you begin to change. Others may not notice as quickly as you feel it, but change is occurring.

We have now explored the importance of taking a step back and considering patterns of narcissistic and emotional abuse. We then explored the challenge and importance of embracing change. We now move into a chapter written by Dr. John Hudson on the importance of humility.

So, It's Not About Me?

Chapter Three: Dr. John Hudson

Do you get this? Is the most important person in your life you? If you fall into the category of men whose needs must come first, you will never succeed in prioritizing your wife in your relationship. Totally impossible. No matter how hard you think you are trying, if you always consider yourself and your feelings first, your wife will never feel or know she is your highest priority.

Do you know what it feels like to be dismissed, set aside, or neglected? Maybe you do because you experienced this in your childhood. More than likely, this is what your mate is experiencing now, and what she's been trying to tell you.

So, the bottom line here is, that it's really not about you (whatever it is on any given day). In fact, more often than not, things happening around you are about everybody else but you. The truth is, if you are struggling with narcissistic traits or tendencies or are an emotional abuser, it's impossible for you to see and care about the people around you. You simply can't figure this out. The reason you can't figure it out is that this is a foreign language to you. Your inability to see yourself and the importance of others is clouded by selfishness and pride.

When and How Did This Pride and Selfishness Begin?

As young boys, we were taught to be "strong". Being strong was respected, but weakness was not– this is a value so many of us were raised with. We were raised to be strong and proud and admired for these traits. Pride and strength are character traits that are often rewarded. Too much pride and no sense of the needs of others is not a strength, though, and can be harmful to those around you. Pride, by definition, puts your needs, wants, and desires ahead of anyone else's. This may have been part of your upbringing, but yesterday's boy is today's man, and being filled with pride, and putting your needs above others, does not work well in today's world.

Maybe you're reading this book and reacting with – 'I wasn't raised to be selfish or prideful'? Could pride have developed because of endless accolades from those around you admiring your abilities, your persona, your successes – even while you were yet in high school?

You might even say, 'I had a good moral, community and service-minded upbringing ... my parents were pillars in the community ... we all served in the community'. Think about it, though, who are you now?

What is your wife's experience with you, not the people at work or outside the walls of your home? What impact did your upbringing have on how you show up today? Realizing the truth of this is critical to overcoming unhealthy attitudes in your relationship with the present.

As you are reading this book there must be some consideration of your childhood and early adolescent years. The question needing to be answered is "How were you raised?" Were you nurtured in healthy ways, neglected, or even taught to fight (selfishly) for your way? What attitudes and behaviors were modeled for you? Were your parents focused on all that was important to them and unable or unwilling to attend to your needs? From this, you developed the understanding that your needs are most important. You learned to fend for number one – yourself!

From the beginning of your childhood, if everything was about you it is because of this selfish, prideful thinking, that it's impossible for you to consider others around you. In fact, this prevents you from even 'seeing' the needs of others – even your spouse.

Furthermore, when your significant other has your best interest in mind and tries to prioritize you – it's impossible for you to comprehend this. You can't believe this because in your mind,

"it's everyone for himself" You must take care of "number one" (yourself) because nobody else will.

Of course, you don't say this out loud because it's not okay to say it. Subconsciously though, you act this out because that's what you've always been taught. Maybe you were pushed or told you had to be responsible for yourself and look out for yourself.

With this kind of modeling as you were growing up, of course, you're going to be thinking about yourself first. You think about protecting yourself; about fending for yourself and about making sure that your needs are met.

When we look at the nine narcissistic traits listed to diagnose Narcissistic Personality Disorder (NPD), PRIDE is an underlying common theme for all nine of these traits. This foundation of pride, culminating in these traits, often becomes the catalyst for Emotional Abuse.

Traits of Narcissistic Personality Disorder

Exhibits an exaggerated sense of self-importance

Has a preoccupation with fantasies of unlimited success, power, brilliance, beauty, or ideal love

Believes he is "special" and can only be understood by, or should associate with, other special or high-status people

Requires excessive admiration

Has a sense of entitlement

Selfishly takes advantage of others to achieve his own ends

Lacks empathy

Is often envious of others or believes others are envious of him

Shows arrogant, haughty, patronizing, or contemptuous behaviors or attitudes.

After reviewing this list, you might be thinking: "Well, I'm not a Narcissist because I don't have all of these traits." Let's be real, you do not have to score a perfect 9 for there to be a problem.

I appreciate Dr. Hawkins when he tells the men working with him "Even a little bit of Narcissism is too much".

Take a moment. Look at the list again. Has your wife, or anyone else, ever mentioned any of these traits to you, about you? Or possibly softened the words and used other terms. For example, have you been accused of not caring for anyone except yourself? This is a combination of self-importance and lacking empathy. If you have any of these traits the results are the same, and you have work to do.

It's really not about how many traits you have, it's about whether you're willing to admit that you have them. This is similar to the situation of someone struggling with addiction. For someone with an addiction, to overcome a problem, they first have to admit that they have a problem. This is exactly the situation you may be finding yourself in now.

In the previous chapter, the emphasis was on embracing the need for change. However, let's be clear, a strategy for change means absolutely nothing if there's no real commitment or understanding of the need to change. You must see the need for change based on an honest review of these traits. If you can't personally be objective enough to see your true self, then you must be willing to embrace the assessment of others.

Each one of the traits listed above requires a unique strategy to overcome it. When you combine the need for change with an understanding of these traits, it is critical for you to begin the necessary work for change to occur.

Once you embrace the possibility you have Narcissistic traits, you are ready to begin the work of implementing change, countering the behaviors and attitudes that emanate from the trait. For example, if you realize now because your wife has said you lack empathy, you can begin the process of changing by studying and understanding empathy.

Maybe at this point, you have a strong feeling of being attacked. Why does it always have to be about you causing the trouble in the relationship? This is completely understandable as you have spent your entire life being strong and right. More than likely your mate is hurting from the years of abuse and recognizes she has very probably contributed to your behaviors by enabling you.   She has now made the decision to seek change and can no longer continue the enabling without losing herself. The most important point in all this is she brought these things to your attention because she cares about the relationship; because she cares about being protected, because she cares about you.

Humility: Understanding What it Means

While it is essential to provide definitions of the terms we are using, it is also necessary to provide a clear understanding. We can clearly define humility but be aware that humility can be easily faked-false humility. It is not that hard to pretend or appear to be selfless when the underlying reason for acting with humility is for selfish motives. For example, being kind and giving gifts with the hope of something in return.

Merriam-Webster defines humility as "freedom from pride or arrogance: the quality or state of being humble". It is not proud or haughty: not arrogant or overly assertive or aggressive. Humility is the quality of being humble and not thinking that you are better than others. This requires lowliness of mind versus haughtiness or arrogance. Again, the definition is clear, it is not proud, haughty, or selfish, all traits typical of a narcissist and emotional abuser or someone with narcissistic tendencies.

Humility is characteristic of individuals who seek to serve others before themselves. Some essential traits of humility include the following:

Being of service to others

Admitting when you are wrong

Acknowledging your own weaknesses

Not being boastful of yourself or your accomplishments

Embracing humility is what allows us to prioritize others and care for them deeply. This encourages us to ensure others are fully attended to before presenting our own wants or needs. In a marriage, we must see the need to lead with humility. This pushes us to attend to our mates with care and love.

However, we've been conditioned to lead with strength and power, which is mostly experienced as powering through or over those close to us – especially our mates. We've been taught to "take charge" and make decisions. This leaves no room for empathy, understanding, and collaboration with your mate. Is this you? Have you been challenged to lead with power and authority? This is neither what your mate wants nor needs. She needs to be included, considered, and even cherished.

Humility is necessary to overcome, or possibly even eliminate, the overwhelming pride that causes narcissistic behavior. It is unlikely you can overcome pride without first fully understanding the negative impact of pride and me-centered thinking. Me-centered thinking is the attitude of focusing on "self" and this became our mantra when we were encouraged to "take care of number one". This also led to the emergence of the self-serving behaviors and attitudes we are experiencing now.

To fully appreciate "humility", it's critical to understand what it is not. The opposite of humility is pride. Let's consider this using an analogy of light and dark. It's been said, that there's no such thing as darkness, it's just the absence of light that creates darkness.

The same can be said of humility and pride. The absence of humility creates pride. Therefore, it's critical for anyone consumed with pride to pursue developing humility. Let me assure you, this will never happen by chance. This effort takes intentionality to develop personality traits associated with humility which were previously non-existent.

This is often seen in the men we encounter at the Marriage Recovery Center. Are you one of these men who are ultra-focused on your own needs? Seeking to be surrounded by others who help meet your personal needs, wants, and desires? The wives of these men have tried for many years to persuade them to see themselves clearly. Your wife needs you to understand how prioritizing yourself destroys your marriage relationship. Wives are tired. They are tired of these self-serving attitudes.

Ed and Sarah came to me with concerns beyond the scope of normal marriage issues. They didn't just have communication issues. Sarah complained of emotional abuse and Ed's attempts to control every decision in their life. She shared how she tried to tell Ed about her concerns but was always told she didn't know what she was talking about. By the time they came to see me, Ed had become callous to anything Sarah had to say.

Ed was an electrician by trade and had grown up in a blue-collar world. His dad taught him from a very young age the importance of hard work and forging his way ahead in life. As a result, Ed worked hard, proving to himself he was a success by building the largest electrical contracting company in the Midwest United States.

Ed was very proud of his accomplishments as a self-made man. So proud, he lost sight of reality and began to worship himself, the creator of his empire. Ed and his work came first, before everything, leaving no room for anyone else in his life, including Sarah and his kids.

By the time Ed and Sarah came to me, Sarah had lost hope. For many years, Sarah had implored Ed to recognize how his pride and perceived 'strength' were destroying their marriage. When they arrived for their first session with me, Ed had all but completed this destruction. Although Sarah's message was clear, Ed could not hear her through his wall of pride. Ultimately, Ed's lack of humility cost him his family.

Importance of Humility

Without question, humility is important in the deep gratitude we hold for others and in our love for them. Humility helps us extend compassion and empathy for others. This is the capacity Ed lacked. Do you lack humility like Ed?

Humility is the key to opening the door to change. Individuals who do not have humility are less likely to accept input from others, especially those very close to them, and implement actions necessary to produce needed change. Humility can be, however, the impetus for a listening ear and empathy for the needs of others.

Humility helps a person receive "feedback" instead of hearing "criticism". Have you been easily offended and aggressively defensive when your wife tries to share some healthy feedback? Subconsciously, you labeled her feedback as unhealthy, unwarranted criticism. You retaliated by accusing her of "attacking you". Can you see where she might have been trying to come to you with her legitimate concerns, and felt dismissed or demeaned by your reactions?

As shared in Sarah and Ed's story, Ed's pride blocked the possibility of him approaching Sarah from a position of humility. If Ed had listened to Sarah's perspective, he would have seen how his behavior and attitudes had crushed her and undermined any desire Sarah had to connect with him.

Why Is Humility Necessary?

Having humility is imperative for you to be able to hear feedback, an important step as you move forward towards a healthy position, ready to implement change. Humility is often characterized as genuine gratitude, a lack of arrogance, and a modest view of oneself. However, humility goes beyond this. You need to be challenged to be humble and trust in the wisdom and insight your wife can provide. True humility is seeing ourselves as we truly are. Its importance cannot be overstated. In fact, getting it "wrong" or misunderstanding the need for true humility will have a negative impact on your spouse and marriage. As you can see, the trait of humility contributes positively to every relationship around you. A lack of humility creates separation.

Humility Strengthens Connection with Other People – Especially Your Spouse

Humility emphasizes care and concern for the people around you and lessens the potential for you to be self-absorbed. In fact, with true humility, your focus turns to the ideas, opinions, and needs of others over those of yourself. Confidence in others can raise your confidence in humanity – therefore, even yourself.

What Does Healthy Humility Look Like in Relationships?

As we have been learning, humility is your willingness to prioritize your spouse ahead of yourself. This is not easy and requires commitment and diligence. It's one of the most challenging things a person must be able to do because it requires sacrificing self-gratification for the needs of other people. A relationship with two people being humble with each other creates mutual respect

Ask yourself this question: Does your spouse believe they are your HIGHEST priority? If your spouse cannot – without hesitation – say 'YES' to this … you have work to do.

What is the Evidence of Humility in Relationships?

Remember the role of humility in your relationships is having the ability to hear feedback and implement change. Individuals who struggle with humility often feel hurt when critiqued or criticized by anyone, but especially by intimate partners. Feedback in a relationship should not be feared or something we get upset over. Individuals who are self-protective are often easily offended when provided feedback. Our husbands/wives are a part of our lives to make us the best version of ourselves. Criticisms should be accepted wholeheartedly and should be used as instruments to improve things in our lives, areas needing to be developed. Here are some traits we should strive for in living a life of humility in our relationships.

Being Open to Unsolicited Advice

Unsolicited advice is inevitable and healthy in a relationship, and it should be accepted with an open mind. Rather than feeling hurt or rejecting the feedback, reflect on that advice, and apply it to your life. The process can be uncomfortable, but it is a very important step to take as you begin implementing and sustaining long-term change.

Conversely, when you give advice to your partner, do it with sincerity. This means you must listen to her input and opinions. Your motives behind providing advice are telling. If your primary thought is to be corrective, you might be locked in a right or wrong/black-and-white mindset. This doesn't allow for other perspectives or the possibility you are wrong. Try putting yourself in your significant other's shoes. Would you feel hurt and offended? Advice should be shared in a calming manner to convey you are giving it with pure intentions.

Admitting mistakes

The statement "nobody is perfect" should be a constant consideration in a relationship. Recognizing we are not perfect takes the pressure off. It's not realistic to expect your partner or yourself to attain perfection. We're all human and we make mistakes. It is important to admit mistakes with a pure heart; getting angry or admitting you are wrong just to get out of a situation is not going to gain you anything. Protecting your ego and not accepting a mistake will just make problems worse.

When you have committed a wrong against your spouse you need to apologize. Suppose you yell at your wife. Of course, she is going to be hurt. It is now your responsibility to apologize. Without a heartfelt, sincere apology the relationship is compromised. Admitting mistakes puts you in the right frame of mind to offer a sincere apology and make amends.

Be observant and value others

Being observant means being intentional about "seeing" your spouse's perspective and valuing their opinions. Clear evidence of valuing your wife's perspective or opinion is when you ask her for this and act on what she shares. What if you don't agree with your wife's perspective? Does this make you right and her wrong? Can you resolve this within yourself to adopt the understanding that in many circumstances, perspectives can be diverse and still appreciated? In fact, opinions and understandings can be different and not be conflictual, just different. The key to overcoming differences is validating one another's perspective and striving for compromise. Your wife needs to be seen, heard, and valued.

Appreciation of your wife's perspective means you are curious enough to ask for her insight. Valuing her opinion is evidenced by taking her ideas into account and acting in response. Trusting and encouraging your wife to share ideas or her opinions shows you value her.

Listen

Listening is an art. Although listening doesn't sound like such a hard thing, it seems difficult because we all want to be heard "first". Keep in mind, if you are not listening, there's a good chance the person you are conversing with does not believe you care about whatever they are sharing. How many times have you found yourself thinking about what you are going to say next while your spouse is still sharing? Were you really listening? The moment you start thinking about your next words, you stop listening. It's impossible to fully listen to what your wife is saying if you're formulating what you intend to say as soon as she pauses or takes a breath.

Being humble means caring enough to focus on what the other person is saying. In fact, in a healthy relationship, couples engage in asking curious questions to better understand what each is sharing. Do you ask questions to connect with your wife for a deeper understanding?

For every marriage, for every person, the strategy to overcome pride and selfishness needs to be slightly different. The strategy must be one that addresses the uniqueness of each person involved.

The Story of Jim

Jim and Wendy came to me in a state of marriage collapse. They stated they had tried all the traditional marriage counseling avenues. They even participated in a couple's retreat and a marriage intensive. Nothing seemed to work!

Jim admitted that he had no idea what was wrong. He provided every material thing Wendy and the kids could ever want. He was very successful in his work and was admired greatly in the business community and at church. He was even on the deacon board! How could he be missing the mark so badly?

Not fully understanding the problems, Wendy sought answers. Wendy read marriage books, watched YouTube videos, and listened to podcasts. Her reading watching and listening helped her understand what she was feeling. She began to understand Jim was selfish and was not hearing her needs. It seemed that everything Jim did was for himself. Wendy's research revealed something she had never considered. Could Jim be a Narcissist?

When we met, I challenged them both to complete our initial assessments with honesty and receive feedback from the assessments with an open mind. This challenge was more directed at Jim. I could see him and recognized his struggle with narcissistic traits. Was it possible for him to take the blinders off? At first, his pride was fully blocking his ability to see the truth. As we continued to engage, I encouraged Wendy to share with confidence and I challenged Jim to hear her – really hear her.

Jim listened. In a moment of vulnerability, Jim saw himself. He began to listen well to the truths Wendy shared with him. When challenged, he set aside his pride, and he could finally hear Wendy.

Jim responded well, dove into the necessary work, and changed.

Although a success story to be sure, it didn't happen overnight. The work of healthy change is often delicate and demanding and takes time and continued effort. Through their continued work together, Wendy and Jim became the success story they'd always wanted.

Can your story be a 'success' as well? What are you willing to do? The power of humility cannot be overstated. Humility is necessary for a healthy change to develop. Patience in developing humility is needed.

However, deciding to change isn't always the beginning.

Without some revelation, we might not see the need for change. Remember, we can't change what we don't know. Furthermore, it's often the case that we don't know what we aren't told. In the next chapter, we'll discuss why we sometimes need to hear from others, especially our spouses, as the understanding of why and the initial instigator for change.

You Can't Change What You Don't Own

Chapter Four: Dr. David B. Hawkins

You've taken a step back, reflecting upon how you got here. By now you've reviewed, ad nauseum, the actions you've taken and not taken that brought you to this place. You've begun to embrace the importance of change. Good work.

This is all good. I repeat, good work, but not nearly enough work. Remember, change is difficult. Really difficult.

Many men don't reach a point of crisis until after their life has crumbled and they scramble to pick up the pieces. Their mate has threatened to leave or, in many cases, has already separated. It has sadly taken a breakdown to create an opening for a breakthrough.

That brings us to this critical chapter—the paramount importance of fully owning change. While it sounds straightforward enough, it is anything but straightforward. Real change, and really embracing change, must be accompanied by utter clarity on what needs to change, and this is no easy feat.

Just this morning I sat with a couple, Jeb and Kallie, who were in immense distress, from years of emotional abuse. She's just asked her husband of twenty years to leave their home.

"I don't understand," Jeb said with obvious irritation. "I'm clueless. How did we get here? Am I really getting kicked out of my home?"

These were such good questions, but ones that couldn't possibly be answered in a moment. What he viewed as a sudden and unexpected situation had been contemplated by her for years.

She knew it was anything but sudden or unexpected.

He wanted a simple, straightforward explanation that might change her mind while she struggled with the enormity and pervasiveness of their situation. Answers would require both weeks, possibly months to fully discover, and then only with deep introspection.

How Did We Get Here?

My meeting with Jeb and Kallie this morning was a critical one. I knew it had taken years to get to where they were, and if Jeb was truly honest with himself, he did too. But, then again, being honest with oneself is no easy matter.

Notice how Jeb framed the issue— "getting kicked out of my home." Perhaps his words slipped by you, but they sure didn't slip by Kallie, as she winced at her husband's words.

He was not being kicked out of their home but was rather being asked to give her space to reflect, breathe, and consider their situation. Consider her words:

"We didn't get here overnight, Jeb," she said. "I've been walking on eggshells with your temper for years. I've held my breath hundreds of times, waiting for you to get angry with me again. I've asked you to go to counseling many times and you always have an excuse not to. I've asked you to own your anger and your intimidation, and you always blame me. I can't take it anymore."

Jeb stared blankly at his wife as she shared her pain. Clearly, he did not fully understand. You see, Jeb really could not see and could not be expected to see it all. He has spent years rationalizing his anger, normalizing his actions. He has used myriad defenses such as minimization and justification to stifle his shame. He had projected his problems onto his wife so he could feel normal, and the cumulative impact on his wife has been enormous. When actions like Jeb's are pervasive and longstanding, it's called *emotional abuse.*

But again, how did Jeb and Kallie get where they are? How did they get here is a question every man in our Core group asks himself, again and again. Temptations to normalize, minimize, and justify actions must be confronted at every turn in order to arrive at the brutal truth.

Clueless

Jeb claims to be 'clueless.' This is a sentiment I've heard from men hundreds of times. How is it possible for so much harm to be done for so long with such horrendous consequences, and yet feel sudden and unexpected? We have a saying in Core Group that goes like this:

"You can't change what you don't own, you can't own what you can't see, and you can't see unless someone shows it to you--and you embrace it."

While this may sound simple enough, remember that men like Jeb don't really want to see their shortcomings. They use countless defenses, an array of self-protective mechanisms, to avoid feeling shame and inadequacy. So, even though these men have been given tons of clues, men fail to put the pieces together until it's too late.

You can hear Kallie's intense frustration:

"I've given Jeb a million chances to change," Kallie said during the session where she announced her need for a separation. "His saying he's clueless is a huge part of the problem."

Yet, he felt clueless, and perhaps that's where you are today as well. Your mate has offered clues—more than clues probably-- for years and is now exhausted from 'over-functioning,' coaching, teaching, instructing, and begging for change. This is not a game. This is her life. Now it's your turn to put the clues together, figuring out what exactly needs to change.

An Intervention/ Time Apart

Jeb and Kallie are both horribly sad as they face a time apart. Not every woman will reach the conclusion Kallie did, to separate, but many women have strongly considered such action. She has wondered how to bring about an intervention that would lead to change. She has wondered, again and again, what she must say or do to bring about change. Life without change, without true ownership of her husband's abuse, is worse than the incredible disruption a separation will create.

Pause and consider what kind of interventions—steps taken to bring about change--have already occurred in your marriage. Has she pulled apart emotionally? Has she stopped confiding in you? Has she pulled apart sexually? Has she threatened to leave? These are 'red flags' indicating something is very wrong.

Whether you have faced a physical separation is not a critical matter—it is whether you and your mate have successfully faced the severity and enormity of the problems. Whether or not you're facing a physical separation, you've undoubtedly faced some kind of disruption of healthy relating.

Interventions, of any magnitude, often bring clarity to a troubled situation. How have you responded to small or large interventions? These are opportunities to listen for clarity, and to put the clues together so you know what must be changed.

A Life Unraveled

Both Jeb and Kallie will now spend the next several months taking an inventory of their lives. It will be very hard work. Their lives didn't unravel this morning. Their lives began unraveling years ago and they both need to spend time reflecting on how that happened.

This perspective is critical. If either focuses solely on this terrible day, they won't be able to find meaning and understanding in their lives.

Rather, they must now step back and see this day as an important piece to a larger puzzle.

Jeb must begin by seeing this day as a culmination of years of entitled actions. He must ask himself, "How could I get to the point of acting with hostility toward my wife, again and again? How could I be so self-absorbed? How could I be so clueless?" The answers to these questions hold the possibility of very important changes.

Likewise, Kallie must now face truths as well. How could she allow herself to be mistreated, again and again? She too has lived with her own denial. She too has used various 'thinking errors' of rationalization, minimization, and justification to normalize wrongfulness. She too is experiencing her own breakdown. Both have immense work to do.

Clearing Away the Clutter

Before embarking on any significant change, you must clear away the clutter. You must become crystal clear about your intentions. This requires acute focus and laser-like intentionality.

Anything less is sure to fail.

How can we think new thoughts, have new dreams, and move in new directions without first having the beginning urge to move in this new direction? How can we make any meaningful adjustment to a radically new direction without making room for these new thoughts?

Whether large or small, you're facing an intervention—a time to reconsider direction. An intervention of any size is a powerful opportunity to embrace new thoughts and change directions. The intervention, however, it has taken place, sets the stage for clearing away clutter and making room for new thoughts.

Is it natural to panic? Of course. But remember that change cannot happen without disruption. Disrupting the status quo leads to more time to focus on critical aspects of life that need to be considered.

Whatever has happened to you, you must create space for new ideas. You will need to step back and consider your priorities. This is a good time to buy a journal so you can reflect on your life. Perhaps you will spend more time in prayer and reflection. Perhaps you will simply sit and stare out the window as you take stock of your life. Again, you must make space for new ideas. You dare not crowd them out with other seemingly 'urgent' matters.

This present task of 'owning your issues' will take enormous focus. You must now make room in your life for therapy, support groups, and accountability partners. 'Clutter' may take the form of many 'important' matters—family, work, chores, leisure pursuits—all good things.

But, again, if you're going to move in a new direction, if you're going to add something new and of great importance to your life, you'll need to make room for it. You'll need to clear away any disrupting clutter. If you make the mistake of crowding this new venture into an already crowded space, the new venture won't last long.

Letting Go of Resentment and Victim-Thinking

Let's revisit Jeb's phrase, *"getting kicked out of my home."* This phrase may have slipped by you, but it didn't slip by me and certainly didn't slip by Kallie. Jeb had a longstanding habit of blaming her for his actions.

Blame—displacement of responsibility—is a dragon that must be slain. This fire-eating monster will threaten Jeb and Kallie, and possibly you, at every turn. Why do I say that?

Blame, you see, has the intention of displacing responsibility. If Jeb holds onto his resentment, he'll rehearse how unfair it is for Kallie to pull away emotionally. He'll minimize his wrongdoing and find reasons to blame her. Their entire marriage hangs in the balance of whether he faces the truth of his situation or not.

Let's compare and contrast *blame* with *ownership:*

Blame says:

- "It's not my fault."
- "I didn't do anything wrong."
- "I'm being unfairly attacked."
- "My problems are normal."

Contrast the above with the voice of *responsibility:*

- "I've brought this situation onto myself by my actions."
- "She is right to separate from me."
- "I must change, making her feel safe and valued."

- "It took immense courage for her to take these actions."

Resentment is the emotion that typically fuels blame and must be challenged. Resentment has been called "resend-ment— resending blaming thoughts again and again." Resentment is fueled by rehearsing thoughts of feeling victimized and refusing to own one's actions.

Resentment is the opposite of growth and forward action. If you indulge in these narrow, limited thoughts, you will cause even more harm and hamper your progress. You cannot afford to indulge in these self-protective, immature thoughts. Your work must include bigger, broader, more expansive thoughts.

Doing His Work

What will it take to get things back on track? Can anything be done to minimize the severity of the breakdown? Most assuredly, yes! But things can get worse and will if you don't do your work.

Doing your work is a central aspect of this book and these chapters are essentially the outline for doing that work.

Doing your work is similar to any project you undertake. Any trip you take, any project you take on, starts with a plan. It all begins with intentionality---a decision to change directions. You anticipate the steps needed to accomplish your goals. The same can be said for 'doing the work.'

But again, you cannot change what you don't own---this again, is a common phrase in our Core Men's Treatment Program. Why? Because until you fully embrace the fact that you have caused harm and must grow, you won't change anything.

As you learned in the last chapter, change cannot occur until you have surrendered. We've discussed the importance of humility, and having a receptive attitude to change. You must be willing to stare into and face the facts, of your emotional abuse. You won't soften the blow by minimizing your actions. You can't displace responsibility or deny your actions. You must face it all.

What are other aspects of the work you must do? You must own patterns of harm and prepare for depth, and character change.

Let's explore what this entails.

Character Change

Jeb is understandably anxious. He is uncertain about what he is being asked to change but is beginning to see that the expected changes cannot be superficial. Rather, his changes must be deep and meaningful.

This seemed overwhelming to Jeb, as it is to all men in our program. What exactly does it mean to do *deep, character work*? I'll lay out some of the issues Jeb and the other men in the group face. Bear in mind, that each of these issues involves long-held patterns of thinking and acting.

Anger Issues: Anger, of course, is a normal emotion. Anger signals us that something is wrong and needs to be righted. However, anger gone astray leads one to spew venom onto another in hurtful ways whenever things aren't going the way we want. This often includes name-calling, put-downs, bullying, and sarcasm. Anger is not shared in respectful ways but is intended to hurt and control.

Defensiveness: Defensiveness is used to stop another person from speaking and is always a central aspect of emotional abuse. It is always wrong and hurtful. Defensiveness takes many forms, including excuse-making, justification, and explanation. At its worst defensiveness becomes argumentative and domineering. Defensiveness is often a way of minimizing one's actions so as to feel 'normal.'

Being Easily Offended: Being 'thin-skinned' and taking criticism personally has no place in a relationship. The man who is 'thin-skinned' argues against criticism. Because many men are 'thin-skinned,' they give off the impression that they cannot tolerate any concerns brought to them.

Projecting Blame: The individual who blames is challenged with owning their part in a problem, focusing instead on what their mate did wrong. Blame stops the other from being heard, and from having their concern brought forward. Rather, the focus is on what their mate has done wrong, exclusively.

Truth Twisting: Truth-twisting is another defensive, avoidance tactic, used to distort what is happening. Truth-twisting occurs when you shade the truth, distort her intentions, or sugarcoat your actions. This may not be a conscious action, but rather a pattern of avoiding facing criticism.

Domination: Domination is an attempt to maintain total control. Domination is typically used to avoid vulnerability and always inhibits personal growth. This may take the form of argumentativeness and badgering, again used to maintain control.

Dismissiveness: Dismissiveness is a pattern of minimizing the truth of another. Dismissiveness involves finding something wrong with what that person is saying as opposed to seeking the truth of their concerns.

These character traits tend to be pervasive and chronic. These are traits we cling to and are hard to change. Can they change? Yes, but complete ownership is the key and is what we refer to when we talk about 'doing the work.'

Breaking Down Self-Protection

With rigid self-protection, complete ownership is impossible. While self-protection is a normal, very human trait, when seeking character change you must seek vulnerability above self-protection, humility above being right.

This is no easy feat. We're all wired to guard against danger, to avoid painful situations. No one wants to feel inadequate, vulnerable, and perhaps even guilty. But that is the path to growth. You must lean into giving up self-protection and trust this process.

Moreover, you will be challenged to focus exclusively on your wrongdoing, not that of your mate. It's natural to focus on the wrongs of another while neglecting our own wrongful actions. These tendencies, woven into our character, however, must be broken down. It won't be easy work but crucial for growth.

Remember Jeb's question, "Am I really getting kicked out of my house?" This question may seem innocuous, but it is filled with self-protection and lacks humility.

No, Jeb, you're not getting kicked out of your house. You're being asked to leave because you have failed to attend to your wife's concerns for years. You're being asked to leave because you've been abusive for years. You're being asked to leave because your wife has been feeling increasingly anxious in your presence. Face the facts, Jeb. You have created this mess and the only way out of it is through it---doing your work!

These are harsh words, to be sure. We might be tempted to feel sorry for Jeb, but this won't serve him well and certainly does a disservice to Kallie. We could side with him, but this would only prolong their problems, making recovery even more difficult.

Jeb must break down his self-protection. He must sit, again and again, feeling sad and vulnerable. He must face the truth of his situation. Anything less will complicate matters and prolong his recovery.

I want to say this again because it bears repeating. The only real path forward is one of honesty and vulnerability. It means Jeb will feel bad, for sure. He will feel lonely, lost, and frightened. He will feel guilty and inadequate. But these vulnerable feelings will allow him a viable path back to his wife. This is his only path. And so, again and again, when he is tempted to soothe his troubles by minimizing wrongdoing, he must face the truth of his situation.

You must do the same. It's hard work, but good work, that leads to the possibility of relating in a healthy way.

Her Work

It is always important to bear in mind that while you are doing your work, she has been, and will continue, to do her work. Men too frequently lose focus, shifting from their work and instead focusing on her work. This is a huge mistake, for several reasons.

First, your focus must remain steadfastly on your work. It is impossible to do your work and be thinking about the work she must do.

Second, she has been doing her work for a long time. She's the one who's been reading books, watching videos, and seeking counseling.

Finally, her work is just that—her work to do. It's actually none of your business. Stay focused.

Jeb is tempted to focus on being asked to leave his home and marriage, feeling unfairly victimized. But, what about Kallie?

What about your mate?

Think about this: Kallie has already been doing a lot of work which has led her to this point. Your wife has likely done the same. Women have typically read far more books, watched far more videos, and have been to far more counseling before the husband begins his work.

Does she still have more work to do? Probably. While it looks different, it is important work.

I often say to women who reach out to me for help, "You must go through your own intervention. You must face the ways you've tried to hold everything together. You must allow your relationship to disintegrate, with the hopes of rebuilding it. You have losses to grieve and must use wisdom regarding the path forward."

She needs to shift her focus. Much of her frustration and anger has been focused on him and now I ask her to continue her work. What has she denied up to this point? How has she attempted to 'hold things together' in spite of horrible obstacles? She will need to reflect and consider the impact of emotional abuse on her and what her current situation will require of her.

Her denial, quite possibly, has been as determined as his. Her efforts to not face the brutal truth have been as powerful as his, perhaps for different reasons.

It is important for you and her to reflect upon the path that has brought her to this point. It is not an event that brought her here, but rather years of mistreatment. She has gone through a rollercoaster of emotions and thoughts, blaming you, blaming herself, and perhaps even blaming God. She has gone through times of thinking she was magnifying the problems, only to be jolted back into the reality of the harm being done to her.

She must also have 'the breakdown that leads to the breakthrough.' She must break down her inclinations of self-protection, relationship protection, and protection of the family.

This is scary work, but so essential.

Women who are married to abusive men often have entrenched patterns of codependency. They are often inclined to hold the family together, having tremendous and understandable fears for their home, children, and family. Their tendency to 'nest' will be massively disrupted.

Additionally, women must face and challenge the threats he has used to intimidate and, the efforts he has used to not take ownership of his problems. She must recognize that if she causes a 'breakdown,' there will be a tremendous ripple effect. Her marriage, family, finances, and home life, all will be impacted---and she will need to deal with these consequences.

Jake and Gradual Ownership

You can't change what you don't own, but ownership is actually a process, not an event. Remember Jake? He entered our Core Treatment Program reluctantly, resisting the process. He entered treatment with a poor attitude, so often the case with abusive men. Ownership came ever so gradually with Jake. He shared the following thoughts near the end of his initial Core group.

"I'm beginning to see my abuse of my wife," he said. "It has been good for me to hear the stories of the other men, although I struggle to see myself as bad as some of them. I suppose

I might be minimizing my problems."

Notice Jake's gradual movement, from externalizing his problems to the beginning of ownership. Therapy, and any change process, is often gradual and perhaps you can see that with Jake.

It is common for the men in our program to appreciate the stories of the other men. They have a sense of not being alone as they watch others struggle to take ownership of abuse. They watch others protect themselves with attitudes of minimizing wrongdoing, blaming their mate, and making excuses for wrong. They are able to see more clearly, when listening to other men, how wrong their thinking has been and the changes that still need to be made.

Notice Jake's words---he '*supposes*' that he has caused harm and wonders whether or not he is 'as bad' as others, though is not sure. He is grappling with owning the severity of his actions. This gradual unfolding of ownership is normal and to be expected, though it must be understood that complete ownership is needed for depth change.

While change is typically gradual, you need complete ownership for real change to occur. Your mate will sense any faltering. They know, intuitively, whether you have taken complete ownership without justification, explanation, or defense.

I have asked many women the following questions:

"When it comes to change, do you need a little change, a moderate amount of change, or significant change and transformation?"

The answer is ALWAYS the same: "*total transformation.*"

This is a critical moment in counseling, for the man *and* the woman. Why? Because her answer establishes the goal she requires. If she needs a little bit of change, she should settle for what she currently sees. If, however, she requires a moderate to significant change, then there is greater enormity to the task facing all of us.

This might feel overwhelming. Total transformation. Significant change. This is no small task and is something for you, your mate, and your counseling team to be very clear about. Your treatment goals dictate the extent and quality of counseling you receive.

Confronting Layers of Denial

Character is a very difficult thing to change. Why? Because character is comprised of longstanding patterns of thinking and behaving and because we have built-in methods for self-protection that keep us safe, and stuck. These built-in layers of protection are patterns of denial, used by all of us to reinforce our view of ourselves and normalize our situation.

"It's not so bad," you say in order to mitigate feelings of shame.

"It's not all my fault," you say to displace responsibility.

"I didn't do it," you say to avoid facing the severity of your actions.

These are all 'thinking errors' and the list could go on and on, for there are innumerable ways of avoiding taking full responsibility. Confronting these many aspects of denial is typically a very challenging task for two reasons: first, we don't want to feel bad, and second, we don't fully recognize that we're doing it.

Confronting patterns of denial is a very difficult process and is one of the reasons that treatment is so challenging. Your treatment provider must be strong enough to challenge you, over and over to take full responsibility for your harmful actions as well as harmful thinking patterns, helping you recognize things you've never realized. Yet, change occurs when, and only when, you clearly see and accept the need for change.

How Much Change Does She Need?

I had a spirited conversation with my colleague, Dr. Lenne' Hunt, our Victim's Treatment Specialist, about the topic of accountability and ownership. We discussed the idea of whether 'his harm was intentional' and how much change most women need to feel safe in a relationship.

Please understand that I was coming from the vantage point of working primarily with men, men who were working hard to grow up and become healthy, working hard to overcome abusive attitudes and actions.

"I see a lot of women who still want their marriage to work," I shared.

Dr. Hunt seemed surprised.

"Oh, I don't," she said. "By the time they get to me they are often D.O.N.E. They've watched him avoid responsibility for years and refuse to fully change."

"Do you think these men are really refusing to change?" I asked.

"The women I work with are tired of half-measures. They see some change, some ownership, but they are tired of being in harm's way," she continued. "They have told their mate again and again what they need differently, only to have their words ignored, minimized, or deflected. They're exhausted. They may see tiny steps of progress, but when they ask themselves if the change is enough to stay in the relationship, they often say it's not."

Her words were sharp and firm. I've heard similar statements from other trauma specialists.

"How can I expect them to stay in a situation where they are triggered, or harmed, again and again?" she asked.

"You make a great point," I said. "These women must make a very difficult decision about whether the changes they see are enough for them to stay."

Dr. Hunt paused, then added more.

"We tell women that they need to decide if they can 'stay well,' and if not, they may need to leave the marriage for their own health and well-being."

Dr. Hunt's words are harsh but real. A little change is rarely enough. A little ownership will not lead to the significant change it takes to have a healthy relationship.

Brutal Honesty

Dr. Hunt challenged me to face the severity and criticality of this work. Real change must happen, now. So, this brings about the question, if partial ownership won't lead to change, what does full, total honesty look like?

We repeatedly teach the five-step approach to ownership:

1. *I did it.* This is a full admission of wrong attitudes and behavior, free from any justification, rationalization, or even explanation. It is a clear admission that describes wrongdoing. For example:

    "When angry I call you horrible names. I walk out while you're talking and tell you you're crazy."

2. *I am wrong.* It is imperative to share that the actions are wrong and why they are wrong.

    "No one deserves to be called names. That is dehumanizing and provocative. To be told you are 'crazy' is violent and abusive. I did that and it is horribly wrong."

3. *I am sorry.* Full ownership involves having a heartfelt admission of wrongdoing, where the victim feels the abuser's remorse.

    "I'm truly sorry. I was wrong and you don't deserve it. I feel bad for how I treated you."

4. *I can see the impact on you.* Fully owning wrongdoing means empathizing with your victim and experiencing to some extent their pain. It means critically inspecting your actions and the impact of those actions on your victim.

    "I can see that your self-esteem has been impacted. You've lost your vibrancy and joy for life. You're tired and at times depressed. You tiptoe around me and worry about my reactions."

5. *Here is what I will do to change and help you recover.* The abuser must have a clear plan of recovery that involves treatment, support, and then maintenance of change. It also involves taking restorative action so the

victim can truly hope for a better life with you, should they decide to stay in the relationship.

Every one of these steps is critical when it comes to full ownership. Missing any of them will lead to an ineffective plan and ineffective recovery which leads to further emotional abuse.

Making Matters Worse

It is important to recognize that failure to take full ownership does not only slow progress but causes further harm. You must bear in mind that your mate deserves your full ownership, and you will not make progress until you are totally committed to change.

Imagine for a moment the man who, upon being confronted with harmful actions, tells his wife she is exaggerating the problem. Not only does he avoid any responsibility, but also shames and blames her for focusing on his wrongdoing.

Is this man simply protecting himself? No. While he is protecting himself, and avoiding ownership, he is also making matters significantly worse by blaming her. He criticizes her actions, deflecting focus from himself.

Most efforts at self-protection also have an aggressive component to them, making them not only self-protective but hurtful to the other at the same time.

I wrote in a previous book, "Dealing with the Crazymakers in Your Life" that defensive maneuvers are often particularly destructive because they are aggressive toward the person trying to get our attention. Our actions are not simply self-protective but are abusive.

For example, telling your mate to *"Leave me alone"* is not simply self-protective, but threatening and aggressive as well. Can you see that?

Therefore, efforts at true, depth ownership and 'growing up' must take into account patterns of behavior used to avoid feeling ashamed and guilty. You must rid yourself of tendencies to protect and really consider the words she is saying. You must also take ownership of defensive, 'crazymaking' patterns. You will probably need professional help to see and own these patterns, but this is very critical work to be done.

Healthy Shame and Ownership

Are you beginning to see how difficult ownership can be? Ownership is difficult. We've all learned to make excuses for our actions. We all vacillate between feeling *'bad'* and mired in shame, on the one hand, and feeling *'good'* and glossing over our wrongdoing. Striking the balance of 'healthy self-esteem' is hard to achieve.

I remember, when I was young, my mother said, "You should be ashamed of yourself," and she was right. Not to be confused with harmful shame, 'healthy shame' is required if we are ever to take full responsibility and ownership of our actions. After all, if we don't 'feel bad' for what we've done and the impact of our actions on others, why would we change?

This issue tends to be a major stumbling block to full ownership. Some psychologists, in fact, believe not feeling healthy shame is *the* reason for narcissism--- the individual is fighting fiercely against feeling bad and thus emboldens themselves with egotism.

It is critical to feel deep remorse for wrongdoing. This is the fuel needed to embark on depth change. Shame, remorse, and guilt over harmful actions provide the impetus for working on 'growing up' and treating others the way they deserve to be treated.

Do you feel bad for your actions? Do you believe you've owned the full extent of harm done? If not, consider what you still need to change to be able to look in the mirror with integrity and honesty. Consider that 'feeling bad' is actually a very important step in your recovery.

Possible Reconciliation

Most women who have experienced emotional abuse face the decision of whether to stay in a relationship or not. She must decide whether there has been enough change for her to 'stay well.' In many cases she will decide to stay, taking a *'wait and see'* posture, and in other cases will decide she simply cannot entrust her heart to someone who is not fully committed to change.

One woman shared this story:

"When my husband entered treatment, I was very skeptical.

I've lived with him for years and have been hurt repeatedly by him. I haven't felt safe for years and his abuse has taken a toll on me. I began to feel more hopeful when he volunteered to enter the Advanced Core Treatment Group, and I saw gradual positive changes. He quit expecting me to celebrate his changes and apologized more quickly when he was wrong and hurtful. I've invited him back into our home, but there's still a question in my mind whether it will work."

Reconciliation is not a 'once and for all' proposition, but rather a gradual process. It is a gradual process of learning new skills, a lessening of harm done with quicker ownership. It involves replacing bad behaviors with good ones, and unhealthy, immature actions with mature ones.

Ongoing Ownership

Ownership is a major step in healing because again, you can't change what you don't own. This cannot be emphasized enough. Any treatment program intent upon making substantial changes must involve the inspection, again and again, of defenses and efforts to avoid taking full responsibility.

This process of rooting out defenses and self-protection mechanisms can feel overwhelming, but also quite rewarding. It can feel threatening to have one's defenses focused upon, but also good to 'grow up' and notice the benefits that naturally come with responsible living and relating.

Your path forward will include ongoing work. There will never be a time when you can relax and coast. In my lengthy time as a psychologist, I've noticed professionally, and personally, that any relaxing leads to lapses in progress.

My therapist once said this to me:

"David, you can spend your energy picking up the pieces and making repairs or use that same energy avoiding problems. Choose wisely."

One way or another I'm going to use energy to create a healthy relationship, and so can you. You can either use your energy to take care of problems after you have made a mess of things, or you can use your energy to avoid issues. If you find yourself *'stepping in potholes'* again and again, and then finding yourself focused on making repairs, you need to consider using that same energy to avoid potholes and creating a healthy, ongoing relationship.

This involves owning your actions, again and again. This involves an attitude of knowing where you are likely to cause harm, how you are likely to cause harm and replacing those actions with healthy relationship-building actions. It also involves quickly owning up so you can get back to healthy connection.

Real change flows from true ownership, and true ownership cannot happen without ridding yourself of patterns of denial. In

In this next chapter, we will review the many patterns of denial that will limit your progress and how to break them, change them, and even obliterate them.

The Many Faces of Denial
Chapter Five: Dr. John Hudson

What is denial? What are we talking about, anyway. Just because I disagree with what my wife is telling me – is that denial? Can't it be we just don't agree? Then again, are you simply disagreeing or rejecting through denial. These are completely different. It's truly okay to disagree – have a different opinion but rejecting your wife's ideas or perspective because you don't like it is denial. For instance, when you don't like a particular food or drink that's disagreeing. If, however, you impose your tastes – 'it tastes amazing, you must like it' – onto your wife, this is a form of denial.

Denial is defined as a "refusal to admit the truth or reality of something (such as a statement or charge)". Let's say you've been presented with clear evidence of your wrong-doing and then flatly reject that truth. This is clearly denial. If you react with a new or contradicting version of the truth, you've graduated from denial to gas-lighting. Projecting a lie to cover up truth (gaslighting) is the most egregious form of denial. You see, your wife was simply attempting to share some reality, and you've reacted by rejecting her desire to share and shamed her with your reactive lies.

Intentional denial is cold-hearted, calculating and oppressive.

Ultimately, then, this rejection pushes your wife to the point of not wanting to share anything with you. All she wanted, was your attention.

How long has your wife been trying to get your attention to help you see the reality of how serious your marriage problems have become? The reality she tried to share was to help, not to tear you down. The value of what your wife needed to share is now lost. Your inability to see her pure intentions, blocked by your pride, have denied the opportunity to grow. Pride keeps you from hearing the truth she tries to share. When you do not listen and hear your wife, she loses trust in you, the relationship now has become an unhealthy marriage. When you consider this cost, can you afford to NOT listen?

Driven by pride, denial destroys emotional connection, sharing of feelings and concerns; and finally, your marriage. Refusing to listen is just one symptom of denial. Denial comes in so many forms. Denial is powerful and overwhelming. This single, crippling behavior can destroy every aspect of your marriage. When denial creeps in, you stop hearing truth. Openness, honesty and transparency are lost. However, the first victim of denial is your wife's voice.

No matter how much she tried to talk to you – even about small things – your pride denied her precious voice. Over the years she tried to approach you over and over … yet, again and again you blocked her heartfelt words with denial. Initially, she shared her frustration with you. However, after denying her voice, she has gradually lost all desire to share anything with you.

Sound familiar? Eventually, she stopped talking altogether.

Along the way, you noticed a change. She may have stopped being "nice" and started shouting. By your shutting her out, you may well have caused her to shut down. She felt quieted, ignored, and finally, rejected. Your wife's frustration ends with her giving up … her voice never heard.

Steven and Nancy came to me for a Couple's Assessment through the Marriage Recovery Center. Nancy was clearly nervous and seemed on edge. She confessed Steven had agreed to the assessment after she had threatened him with a separation. This was her last attempt to get him to understand the source of their marriage struggles. Steven appeared aloof and distant; he sat detached, staring blankly. Without saying a word, he made it clear he'd rather be a thousand other places than in our meeting.

Frustrated with Steven's attitude, Nancy began, "You have to help us. You have to help Steven see reality." Tears filled her eyes as she looked at Steven, asking, "Why can't you listen – why can't you see?"

When Steven continued with his detached attitude, not even flinching at her words, she said, "I've tried everything to fix the problems in our marriage. Steven will tell you – 'there isn't anything wrong' or that 'I am never satisfied' – that 'he can't ever do anything right'. I've been trying to get Steven to understand how much I'm hurting because of our troubles. Your YouTube videos have been helping me so much, but he won't watch them with me. He just tells me that I'm expecting too much. I'm so tired of his denial."

Just then, Steven almost came out of his chair, pinning Nancy with his posture. "You only see the problems in *our* marriage, we don't have half the problems Bill and Emily have!" For the first time since beginning the Assessment, Steven spoke to me, "Dr. John, it's not me. You must believe me when I tell you she NEVER has anything positive to say about ANYTHING?"

At this, Nancy could no longer hold back her tears. Steven plowed on – "now, look at that … there she goes with the waterworks". Without warning, Nancy screamed, "You deny everything!"

This was all very common. I've heard this music and seen this dance before. Does this sound familiar to you too? Have you rejected your wife's perspective? Your strategy to block her ideas is why you've ended up in where you are in your relationship. Your denial.

Denial in marriage is a common problem that can affect both partners and the quality of their relationship. Denial can take many forms, such as refusing to acknowledge a problem, minimizing its impact, rationalizing it away, or avoiding seeking help for it.

Denial might seem like a good coping mechanism to avoid pain, fear, shame, or conflict, but it will more likely prevent you and your spouse from addressing the root causes of your issues and finding a solution. There are a lot of clear signs of denial – if you are open to seeing them. Are you ready?

As mentioned before, Denial comes in many forms and it's just as true there is plenty of evidence of its existence. First, let's investigate personal denial that affects all relationships in your life. Later, we will discuss denial specific to your marriage and the impacts there. Although we can't cover everything in such a small section of this book; here are some signs that you may be in denial in your personal life:

You feel unhappy, depressed, or anxious most of the time.

You have frequent arguments or conflicts that never get resolved.

You avoid talking about sensitive topics or expressing feelings and needs

You blame others or external factors for your problems - You feel disconnected, lonely, or resentful in your relationship

You notice a decline in intimacy, affection, or trust - You engage in unhealthy behaviors, such as substance abuse, gambling, or infidelity

You ignore or rationalize the consequences of your actions on yourself, your partner, or your family.

If you don't recognize any of these signs, you are in denial. However, if any of these situations ARE evident – possibly the people around have shared them with you – now is the opportunity to address them. Dealing with, understanding and overcoming denial is very difficult. If you're locked down by denial in your life, the road to recovery is long. Even if you initially agree to address these issues, it's all too easy to slip back into denial. The REAL problem comes if you can't or won't, recognize these signs.

Denial is a persistent problem and prevents you from facing the reality of your situation and addressing the issues affecting your relationship. Denial leads to emotional distance, bitterness, resentment, mistrust, and unhealthy patterns of behavior.

Maybe in your case you've learned to disguise or hide the truth because this 'keeps the peace'. Actually, what you are doing is avoiding reality when it benefits you to do so. You aren't keeping the peace; you are keeping YOUR peace. You lie or deceive because it's just a 'white lie'. This little lie – that you tell yourself doesn't matter – doesn't hurt anyone. In fact, though, denial eats at your marriage – one trivial lie at a time.

We looked at the signs of denial above. Because denial is just, well denial, it is often difficult to understand where our need for denial is coming from. Consider the following statements, common reasons people use denial. Do any of them trigger possible truths for you?"

You are …"

afraid of the consequences of admitting the truth, such as harmful behavior or attitudes.

ashamed of your own actions or feelings and seek to avoid responsibility or healthy criticism.

overwhelmed by the complexity or severity of the problem and feel helpless or hopeless to change it. - attached to an unhealthy image or expectation of yourself, your partner, or your marriage, and do not want to admit it. - coping with stress, trauma, or grief, and need some time to process your emotions. Let's dive deeper into each of these reasons.

Fear is often the instigator of denial. Fear can drive you to protect yourself. Many times, in response to fear, we react to situations in ways to protect or to deny the truth being presented by those around us. The added reality of consequences complicates this even further.

If you know your behavior and attitudes have been harmful; you likely also know there are consequences to owning up to these unhealthy patterns. The individual who denies real issues because of fear is usually hopeful those whom they've hurt will simply forgive them or ignore the problems. You may think if you hold someone off long enough with denial – they'll give up and give in.

If you are experiencing the fear that drives you to hide behind denial, ask – why? Why do you protect yourself? Why can't you take responsibility? Why is it too hard to be wrong? Why are you running? Why are you unwilling to accept reality and embrace the need for change?

Shame founded in embarrassment can be healthy. Healthy shame pushes you to learn while denial convinces you it's better to hide. It might be easier, but it's definitely not healthier. However, shame-based denial is not. These are fundamentally opposed.

Shame-based denial pushes you to hide or deny the truth. Maybe you've told yourself – if we just ignore the problems presented and 'move on' we're better off. This is the lie that you've hidden behind because it helps you avoid and responsibility or consequence. All you've done is put off the inevitable. Eventually the truth of circumstances will catch up to you. This is likely exactly why you are reading this book right now.

In the struggle with shame-based denial, you are probably asking yourself – how can any type of shame or embarrassment be healthy. You can't see any benefit to 'confessing' your unhealthy behaviors or attitudes. This might show weakness. However, we're not talking about weakness here. We're actually challenging you to be vulnerable.

If the embarrassing feeling motivates you to pursue personal change, everyone wins. Everybody loses if you don't.

Healthy shame is that which helps us understand the pain you've caused another person and instigates empathy. As mentioned earlier, if you've never been taught the value and importance of empathy, this will be foreign to you. Understand this – healthy shame is a natural and appropriate emotional response that helps us recognize and take responsibility for our mistakes, shortcomings or transgressions. It is an adaptive emotion that motivates us to correct our behavior, make amends, and strive for personal growth and improvement. When we do something wrong, healthy shame is what makes us want to make amends for the person we have offended or hurt.

Shame is not a bad emotion; it can be a healthy one. Having the appropriate level of shame also helps you desire to make repairs when an action has caused harm in a relationship. It pushes us to identify our problem behavior and accept responsibility and accountability for our actions. When others see you experiencing some degree of shame, they will promote empathy and care for you. Then, instead of resorting to unhealthy defensiveness, our defenses usually retreat, and healing conversations can take place.

Overwhelmed? Denial creates or covers up multiple problem behaviors in your marriage until the entire situation becomes overwhelming. The resulting frustration freezes you. You've covered up so many issues with denial you don't even know where to start. Your wife needs everything to change, but you feel so overwhelmed knowing you can't solve every problem today even though you try, so you just give up.

Perhaps your spouse has too many varied, unspoken, or unclear expectations. This confusion causes you to freeze, become exasperated, or give up because you don't understand your wife's requests or needs. Your unwillingness to ask for clarification only complicates everything more. Sure, it's possible you don't understand the needs of your spouse. However, it is more likely to become chaotic because you aren't listening or asking her for help.

It's easier, but certainly dismissing, to ignore your spouse's valid requests. These unhealthy practices lead to the unhealthy image you have of your relationship. The more you don't "ask for directions", the harder it gets to connect. She is ready to share – are you willing to lay down your selfish pride and invite her to share with you?

These reasons for denial, fear, shame, feeling overwhelmed, self-image and stress/trauma/grief might 'feel' healthy and helpful in the moment, but they really create obstacles to personal realizations and growth. The old saying 'the truth will set you free' really applies here. While you will not be freed of responsibilities or consequences, you can become free from the burden of burying problems in your relationship. Free from the burden and stress of hiding.

Denial will impact your more intimate relationships, especially your marriage, in much more devastating ways. As opposed to the denial presented earlier which primarily impacts you as an individual, denial in your marriage has the potential to destroy two people and your marriage. When denial persists in habitual ways with the purpose of avoiding reality presented by your spouse, the negative impacts cannot be easily overcome or corrected.

Some clear signs that denial exists in your marriage are as follows:

You refuse to acknowledge or discuss problems presented, even when there is clear evidence or feedback from your wife.

You rationalize, minimize, or justify the problem, or blame your wife for issues.

You act as if everything is fine; but, ignore or suppress your own or your partner's feelings.

You isolate yourself from your wife (and possibly your children) or seek distractions or escapes from any problems presented to you.

You lie, omit, or hide information from wife or have secrets or lead a double life.

The bottom line is that the same impacts exist when denial in present in your marriage relationship as what we presented earlier for the individual. However, in the marriage, the impacts cause ripple effects for you, your spouse and children, and extended family. Therefore, the fallout is much more serious. Eventually it can become so destructive that even you can see – if you're looking – what denial does.

When you get to the place of understanding the impact of denial in your life, on your spouse, you can see the ripple effect on other relationships. The problem of denial in your marriage does NOT end in your marriage. Your children are pushed away, and extended family become weary of your unhealthy behavior and attitudes. Can you see the signs? They've stopped calling, connecting and even coming around.

Very few people recognize the problem of denial in themselves. Most of us become aware of our denial because someone who cares about us is being hurt by our actions, and our relationships are suffering. It's been said – "we don't know what we aren't told". It must become your goal to become self-aware enough to see your use of denial clearly or seek your spouse's insight.

Once you reach that point of recognition, here are some practical strategies to use as you foster a way forward to address denial.

Understand Denial

Again, denial may be serving as a coping mechanism for you to avoid stress or conflict. You might be ignoring issues in relationships because you fear confrontation or want to maintain the relationship as is. Recognize that denial might be a learned response from earlier experiences.

Check In with Yourself

Pause and breathe deeply. Slow down enough to identify the emotions you feel. Reflect on why you might examine issues in your love life. What is going on? What responsibility do you need to own? Make sure you are willing to remain objective with yourself and your wife.

Talk It Through

Share your feelings with someone you trust. Consider whether you have any irrational beliefs surrounding your denial. Write down your thoughts and feelings.

Seek Support

Join a support group where you can connect with others facing similar challenges. Consider seeking professional help from a therapist or counselor.

Are you ready to change? Denial can be overcome with honesty, courage, and commitment. Although your marriage is unique, there are some steps you can take to deal with denial in your relationship.

Acknowledging the problem and its effects on your marriage is the first step you must take. Are you willing to listen to your wife? Encourage her to be honest with you about what is bothering her and how it is affecting your relationship. It's imperative you resist defending yourself. Don't make excuses or justify your behavior. You must accept responsibility for your part in the problem and be willing to change. Once you can acknowledge there are problems, you are ready to begin talking clearly about everything going on.

So, the next step is communication. It's time to be open and respectful with your partner. Learning to listen to your partner's perspective and feelings without judging, interrupting, or getting defensive is key at this point. When you have been stuck in denial, this is hard to change. It's time to trust your wife's lead. She knows what she needs and wants to share it with you. After you have listened to her … when you have fully heard her, then you have the opportunity to implement needed changes in response.

Ultimately, if you are in denial about problems or concerns in your marriage, it is critical you seek professional help from a therapist or counselor. However, not just any therapist can help you identify the root causes of your denial, explore the impact of this on your relationship, and guide you to overcome your denial and face the truth. You must connect with experts who fully understand the dynamics of denial and the impact, someone who specializes in relationship struggles.

A therapist can also help you and your partner communicate effectively, resolve conflicts, rebuild trust, and strengthen your bond. Denial can be a problem in marriage, but it can turn into an opportunity for growth and healing when its recognized and proper changes are implemented to institute honesty and transparency. There are a few necessary steps – when engaging with a professional counselor – that need to be taken.

Step 1 - Seek professional help. This might seem obvious; but too many times I meet people who are still "talking about doing something", yet they haven't taken any action. Sometimes, denial is too deep or complex to deal with on your own. You may need the guidance and support of a therapist, counselor, or coach to help you identify and overcome the underlying causes of your denial and work on improving your relationship. A professional can help you develop new skills, strategies, and goals to cope with your challenges and enhance your marriage.

Step 2 - Take action and follow through. Once you have identified the problem and its solutions, you need to take action and follow through with your plan. Set realistic and specific goals and monitor your progress. Celebrate your achievements and reward yourself and your partner for your efforts. Be consistent and persistent in your actions and don't give up when you face difficulties or setbacks. Remember that change takes time and patience.

Step 3 - Seek support from others. You don't have to deal with denial alone. You can seek support from your friends, family, or other people who have gone through similar situations. Join a support group, online forum, or community where you can share your experiences, feelings, and tips with others who understand what you are going through. You can also read books, articles, or blogs that offer advice and inspiration for overcoming denial and improving your marriage.

Step 4 - Develop Transparency. Sharing everything in your life with your spouse is the key to intimacy and overcoming denial. This can be one of the most difficult action steps. Maybe you've never been able to be transparent because it felt too dangerous. As I said earlier in this chapter, transparency and honesty require a certain level of vulnerability and this can be real obstacle.

Step 5 - Finally, Sustain the effort to grow and learn. Slipping back into denial will destroy any progress you make. Denial in marriage can be a serious obstacle to your happiness and well-being, but it can also be an opportunity to grow and strengthen your relationship. By facing your problems, communicating with your partner, seeking help, taking action, and seeking support, you can break free from denial and create a healthier, happier, and more fulfilling marriage.

Overcoming denial as a defense mechanism can be challenging, but it's essential for personal growth and well-being. Remember, though, without going through the steps above and striving for change, you'll struggle to overcome it. Remember, overcoming denial requires courage and self-awareness. By addressing it, you can create a stronger foundation for your relationship.

Eventually, Nancy gave Steven an ultimatum. Nancy had already been connected with the Marriage Recovery Center for over a year. Steve knew his wife had changed; but he didn't understand how. Nancy began individual counseling after completing the Redeemed Group for women. Her resiliency grew to a point that she was no longer willing to tolerate Steve's attitudes and behaviors.

Nancy now fully understood the unhealthy power of denial. She found the courage to confront Steven. Once again, Nancy presented her concerns to Steven – especially regarding denial.

And, once again, Steven denied that he was in denial.

Steven finally agreed to a Couple's Assessment. Through this assessment, Steven was confronted with the truth. He could not hold onto denial and his marriage at the same time. Through Nancy's undying efforts, Steven finally agreed to fully participate in the individual work (counseling) necessary.

Owning Your Shadow
Chapter Six: Dr. David B. Hawkins

"How could he do that? How could someone who says he loves me act the way he does?"

How are you capable of emotionally abusing your mate? These are good questions and deserve a deep, intensive and fearless inquiry. It's a search that, frankly, you must do because your wellbeing, and the wellbeing of your mate and those you love, depend upon it.

Why is this issue so critically important? Because depth change requires being boldly honest with all aspects of your character---and that includes your shadow.

We all have a shadow part to our personality—hidden parts of ourselves that still influence our actions, making us capable of harming others. We are all comprised of good and bad traits, and if not fully integrated and transformed, we can act in ways we regret.

For as much as we're capable of loving, kind actions, we're also capable of harmful actions. We've got to be honest with ourselves about this. In the shadows of our lives, we are capable of harsh and sometimes abusive actions. Only a fearless exploration into your shadow side and blind spots will allow you to understand yourself and transform those darker qualities into redeeming ones.

So, let's get started.

Your Shadow

"Those that don't own their shadow are destined to be controlled by it." This quote, attributed to the renowned psychoanalyst, Carl Jung, suggests there are parts of us capable of causing harm, and if we don't recognize them, and harness them, we will cause even more harm.

Whether you call this part of you 'a shadow,' is not critical. What is critical is that you accept, and determine to work on, the part of you that causes harm.

While we are capable of doing wonderful things, we are likewise capable of causing harm. We say things we regret. We do things we regret. We make decisions which we later wonder why we acted the way we did.

Let's agree to call hidden parts of ourselves our 'shadow', and let's agree that we need to uncover these parts, discover these parts and help these parts recover and be transformed. Let's agree that we need to shine a bright light on our darker side, take full ownership of our darker side and embark on a journey of healing our darker side. To not do this work, to remain in denial, means we are choosing to remain naïve and simply hope we won't cause harm again—a fools' errand.

Really Owning Your Shadow

Since we all have a shadow, it's time to own it. What does really owning your shadow entail? Here are a few practical considerations:

Know that your shadow is hard to fully see and own.

You live and breathe in your conscious mind, your "everyday" mind where you are generally calm and well-intentioned. In this 'state' you have every intention to do good, you have lofty ideals and see yourself in a most favorable light. It takes intentional focus to pry into your darker side and explore less favorable intentions.

Appreciate efforts at self-protection working against knowing your shadow.

You have self-protective mechanisms (denial) that protect you from seeing your darker sides, but also keep you stuck. Notice how, when clearly wrong, you minimize, rationalize, blame-shift and 'play the victim,' in an effort to not fully see how destructive you can be. Growth requires you to lift the veil and explore your harmful intentions.

You will likely need help understanding your shadow.

This is hard, hard work. The 12 Step Program of Alcoholics Anonymous calls this work a "Fearless Moral Inventory." In our Men's Core Program, we help men fully own their destructive tendencies and actions. We challenge men, again and again, to not sugarcoat wrongdoing, but rather explore the intensity, history and pervasiveness of harmful actions and attitudes.

Owning your shadow is ongoing work.

Owning your shadow side is ongoing work and you need to cultivate an attitude of self-exploration and growth, always mindful of tendencies toward self-protection and denial. You must stick with the work. You won't regret it.

Transforming your shadow is emotional and spiritual work.

You can do a lot with intention and willpower, but true character transformation is also a spiritual practice. Scripture tells us, "A good man brings good things out of the good stored up in his heart, and an evil man brings evil out of the evil stored up in his heart. For the mouth speaks what the heart is full of." (Matthew 12: 34)

So, to transform your shadow requires not only emotional work— plumbing the depths of your attitudes and behaviors—but also exploration into your heart. This, again, requires brutal honesty.

Core Self/ Protective Self

Another way to go about discovering your shadow is to get to know your Protective Self---that part of you that fights, flights, and freezes in the midst of conflict.

One way to think about your personality is to consider you have three parts: Your Core Self, which includes your Most Vulnerable Self, and your Protective Self. When you are functioning in a healthy way, from your

Core Self, you are aware of your feelings and utilize them to make healthy contact with yourself and others. Life flows relatively smoothly.

When threatened in any way, another part of you comes to the rescue. In this heightened state you shift into a more primitive aspect of yourself, your Protective Self, which takes the expression of fighting, fleeing or freezing.

There is nothing right or wrong about your Protective Self. It is perfectly natural to have developed a coping mechanism that now does more harm than good. What we want to do is become more aware of these tendencies, why they were developed and make healthier choices about them.

Imagine a time when you are hurt by something your mate said to you, perhaps when they were blunt or harsh. Perhaps it's a time when your mate was angry with you for something.

"You're selfish and self-centered," she says. You wince at her words, feeling hurt and irritated. You immediately react, not taking time to process this event.

"How can you call me selfish after all I do for you and our family," you react defensively. You don't stop there, however.

"You're the one who's selfish," you continue.

Without thinking your Protective Self has jumped into action, making matters so much worse. The fight is on.

Now pause and imagine a very different scenario. This time you sit with your hurt and irritation, letting your feelings settle. You comfort yourself, reminding yourself that you will feel better in a few minutes. You take a few moments to reflect on her words. You don't react, but rather take a few moments to nurture yourself and consider how to respond effectively. This is a challenging moment, to be sure, but in your Core Self you know how to effectively respond.

After sitting with your feelings, you deliberate about whether anything needs to be said. Maybe it does and quite possibly it doesn't. Perhaps you choose to respond.

"Ouch, your words stung me," you say, "but I can understand why you said them. I've been selfish and self-centered and I'm sorry for that."

To function this effectively takes a great deal of self-control and maturity. Again, let's imagine what might happen if your Protective Self jumped into your rescue.

"You can't talk to me that way," you snarl. "You're the selfish one. It's time you looked in the mirror."

Your Protective Self—that part of you that rushes in to defend you---has certainly protected you AND is going to cause all kinds of destruction. This kind of self-protection brings a horrendous price tag.

Denying Your Shadow Self/ Protective Self

You might have the mistaken belief that uncovering, and transforming your Protective Self would be easy work. That is far from true since we expend so much energy keeping this aspect of our personality hidden.

It is critical to understand that your Shadow/ Protective Self, is hidden and wants to remain hidden. Because we generally feel ashamed of this part of our personality, we use any number of protective mechanisms, defenses to gloss over wrongful actions. We commonly use defenses such as minimization, denial, rationalization and other defenses so as to not fully own and explore our Protective Self.

I had a challenging conversation with a Core Group member recently in an effort to explore his Protective Self. His wife sent me a note telling me her husband could be brutal when he became angry. She was afraid of him and had issued an ultimatum that unless his angry, Protective Self was transformed, she had no intent to stay married and a separation was imminent.

"Tell me about this angry part of you," I suggested during one group. "She has called you a bully."

"Well, I don't call it anger and I'm sure not a bully," he said. "I call it passion. I can be outspoken and direct."

"Your wife calls it anger and she's afraid of you when you're angry," I confronted.

"She is more soft-spoken that I am and is easily threatened by lots of people," he continued, very defensive. "I'm not a bully."

"Well, we have a problem," I said. "Notice that if you decide to call your Protective Self passionate, you're not likely to change much. If you don't delve into the part she calls a bully, then she won't feel safe and she will likely leave you."

"What do you want?" he continued, becoming increasingly agitated (threatened). "I really think it's her problem and she needs to figure out I'm not the bully she claims."

Can you see how this man hides from the discomfort of calling himself angry, a *bully*? Can you see how stuck he is and how he is digging himself into a deeper hole? Unless he courageously explores this aspect of his nature, his 'blind spots,' his Protective Self, will protect him but at a great cost.

Exposing Your Protective Self

Do you remember Jake? He had a well-developed, destructive, argumentative Protective Self. When Jake felt threatened, insecure or inadequate, his argumentative, Protective Self, rushed in to save the day.

"I don't like to admit it," Jake began slowly, "but I know there's a part of me that can do a lot of damage. When I feel threatened by my wife, I can always muster up an argumentative, all-knowing side to make her back down. I just didn't realize my domineering side caused so much destruction. My wife never wants to argue with me because she knows I will over-power her. I'm starting to realize this argumentative side protects me, but it's not really helping me."

This is good news for Jake. Why? Because he is beginning to create a chasm between himself and his argumentative side, a beginning awareness of the protective, and destructive, power of this part. As long as he remains unaware of this part, he and those he cares about are in trouble.

Jake has done a lot of work to expose and understand his hidden, Protective Self, and it has not always been easy work. Efforts by his wife to expose this dark, shadowy side of his personality had been denied, minimized and even turned on her for the longest time. Exposing Protective Selves is hard work for everyone.

How can you discover and uncover your Protective Self? It isn't impossible, at least once you are intent on exposing it. Here are some questions to help you uncover this shadowy aspect of your personality:

What are you like when you are triggered, threatened, or hurt?

What are you like in your worst moments, actions, and attitudes you might be ashamed of?

Do you tend to fight, flight, or freeze?

What longstanding patterns do you have when upset?

Are you willing to explore this 'protective' part of your personality?

Take a few moments to journal and look over your answers to these questions. Can you see how these questions can lead you to exposing your Protective Self and understanding it, making it easier to transform these qualities?

Remember that your Protective Self is trying to protect you but does so in ways that cause harm. Remember that when we 'fight, flight, freeze' we say and do things that cause harm in the relationship. As you uncover this Protective Self, explore and understand what purpose this part serves. Find out what this part is trying to do. How is this part trying to help you and discover new and healthier ways to get those needs met?

Your Worst Day

Jake is beginning to understand and own his Protective Self, but to really own it, to really understand it, he must get to know it very, very well. He must consider what he is like when his defenses are down, when he is vulnerable, threatened.

For Jake, and you, to really get to know your Protective Self you must be keenly aware of what you are like on your worst day, and that is exactly what I'm asking you to do. Reflect on what you are like on your worst day, when you have behaved badly, a day you want to strike off the calendar. You hate your actions on that day so much, in fact, that you've blocked much of it out of your memory. You haven't reflected on it or spent time learning from it.

You've run from it.

Now, do the opposite. Write about an event where you acted so badly you want to erase it from your memory. After you have finished writing, describing your actions in detail, look at it again with an open heart and a critical eye to see how you have minimized your actions. Examine how you used defenses to 'soften your actions.' Again, this is a time to get to know this shadow part to your personality.

It is critically important to understand what you have done and after that, explore why you have done it. Remember, there are many things to be learned in these events. Draw close to it. How might your spouse describe you on those 'worst days, worst moments?' What were you like? Name the qualities fully and without explanation. What was the issue and why did you react so harshly?

It is likely that as you explore these 'worst days' you will discover they are not isolated events, but rather form a picture, a pattern. It is likely that you have acted in such a way many times. What are the thoughts that fuel such actions? Where did you 'learn' to act the way you do, to think the way you do? What are your wounds that need attention which may be part of your overreaction?

Exploring Your Protective Self

In certain instances, our Protective Self can become a normalized but extreme aspect of our personality. In fact, some theorists believe we are capable of creating a sub-personality---a part of us that thinks and behaves irrationally, completely different than are 'normal' selves.

This is why there is so much talk about a '*Dr. Jekyll and Mr. Hyde*' personality, which originally came from the book by Robert Louis Stevenson titled *The Strange Case of Dr. Jekyll and Mr. Hyde.*

In this fascinating book, Dr. Jekyll is a kind and respected English doctor who has repressed, evil urges inside of him. In an attempt to hide this, he develops an elixir he believes will effectively compartmentalize his dark side. Ingesting this serum works for a time, but eventually, Dr. Jekyll's dark side becomes stronger, and he is unable to control the physical and mental manifestation of his evil personality, Mr. Hyde.

Sadly, and perhaps tragically, this story has become a real experience for far too many victims of narcissistic and emotional abuse. Many men have an all-too-developed 'darker side' which they deny, minimize and try to 'push down,' only to have it rise uncontrolled when triggered. This hidden and often denied shadow often has its own thoughts, beliefs, attitudes and actions.

Remember Jung's words: "Those that don't own their shadow are destined to be controlled by it," and the Apostle Paul said much the same: "I don't want to do what is wrong, but I do it anyway." (Romans 7: 19-25)

Your work, your recovery, must include work on exposing and understanding your 'darker side.' You must bring it all into the light where it can be fully acknowledged, understood and ultimately healed. As you bring your shadow into the light you can make much better choices about how you want to respond to stressful situations.

Dis-integrated!

We can all imagine what the Apostle Paul felt---I do what I don't want to do, and don't do what I want to do. It's so frustrating and can lead to feeling very dis-integrated, fragmented and torn. You might find yourself utterly bewildered by how you act when dysregulated. Your work is to make peace with these differing and warring parts-the part that wants to do well and does, and the part that wants to do well and doesn't. You must sit again with the question, 'How can I view myself as filled with virtue only to act aggressively?'

Integrity means living consistently with the good and bad parts of your character. We know the feeling of having different parts and having those parts war within us. It can feel very disquieting.

If integrity is feeling 'at one,' and living cohesively and consistently, we all know the feeling of living at odds with ourself—or ourselves. We know the feeling of having different parts and having those parts war within us. It can feel very disquieting.

Every man who behaves badly has this disquieting feeling inside. These men feel the haunting presence of different, disintegrated parts, differing, warring parts. Those parts need attention. They are clamoring for attention.

The answer is not to push the noise down, but rather to bring it to the surface. Spending time with the warring parts can lead you to integration, acceptance and possible healing of those parts.

Hidden, Unhealed Wounds

This all leads us again to the topic of healing. We all need healing. We all have wounded parts, trying desperately to protect us. Our efforts at protection—to fight, to flight, to freeze---only make matters worse and don't bring healing.

You must always bear in mind that your Protective Self is trying to protect you. Why? How? Well, we have wounds that are triggered by others. Perhaps they remind us of feelings of inadequacy as a child. Perhaps we're feeling those same feelings we felt from a harsh parent so many years ago. Wounds that are unhealed get triggered by others.

In a sense, we're saying to others, "I won't let you hurt me. I'll fight, or flight, or freeze, but I won't sit here and be hurt." And so, we don't. Wounded earlier in our lives by others, we have made an unspoken vow to 'never be hurt again,' or at the least, to protect ourselves.

This protection, however, this overreaction, is not simply a response to the here and now, but a cumulative response. It's like responding to all the people who have ever hurt you. Ultimately, your reaction is a failure to simply feel what is happening in the present moment.

Let's revisit Jake, his defensive blaming of his wife, resistance, anger, and yet gradual progress.

His wife called him 'selfish and self-centered.' That hurts, right? However, Jake doesn't just sit with his hurt, nurturing himself and choosing how to respond. He reacts from his Protective Self to fight his battle, making matters so much worse. He doesn't sit with his emotional pain—he reacts. He is disintegrated, hurtful, and even vengeful.

Jake has reacted like this for years, long before he met his wife. Jake discovers power in his dominance and uses it to protect himself. It's not working. His Protective Self doesn't help him heal old wounds but only serves to aggravate them.

Healing Wounds

What does healing our wounds look like? Your work is challenging. You must slow everything down and go on an inner journey to discover your protective parts and the wounds they protect. You must bring a healing presence to them, a caring awareness that seeks to nurture yourself.

Pushing our pain away doesn't work---remember Dr. Jekyll and Mr. Hyde. Remember the Apostle Paul. As uncomfortable as it is, you must face your shadow sides.

It is from this authentic space, that you are able to be fully present with others, even those who hurt you. From that mindful place, where you face all your parts, you choose to stay in the conversation or gently take a break, to listen and empathize or step away, temporarily.

Ultimately, we must all do 'healing work' where we slow everything down and bring compassion to our pain. You must ask your Protective Self to step aside so you can caringly explore your wounds. This is daring and powerful work. This work involves grieving over wounds you've carried for some time. It may even involve wounds occurring now in your current relationship.

Notice that your focus here is YOU. Though others can challenge you, you are the one who needs to look within. You are the one who needs healing. This is your work to do.

Here is another invaluable exercise for your healing expedition, seeking to understand your wounds and how you act when wounded. This exercise is called RAIN—an acronym for *Recognize, Allow, Investigate, and Nurture*. Practice each of these steps every time you are triggered, threatened, or tempted to fight, flight, or freeze. RAIN goes like this:

Recognize: Take time to notice what has threatened you. What are you hurting about and how are you handling this hurt? Is it a familiar hurt, something that has happened again and again? How are you responding? Are you fighting, running away, or freezing? Get to know yourself.

Allow: Spend time sitting with your discomfort. Allow yourself to sit quietly and embrace your troubled feelings. Quell any temptation to blurt out feelings or withdraw into silence. Take space and allow your experience to become larger inside you.

Investigate: Seek to understand your experience. Be curious about what has threatened you. Welcome your reaction and let yourself know you are safe, and you want to know what this experience can teach you. This may be a time to journal your experience or talk someone you trust and care about.

Nurture: Give yourself credit for exploring the depths of this issue. Acknowledge the challenge of sitting with your feelings.

Be thankful that you have had the experience and consider any 'takeaways' you have discovered.

Doing the RAIN again and again, will grow your ability to learn about yourself. Done over and over, you will become more familiar with your actions and reactions and your shadow side/ Protective Self will diminish.

Speaking Up for Your Self

Everyone needs an advocate, someone who encourages us, challenges us, and notes our progress, and this must be YOU. This may seem counter-intuitive, because you have likely been shouting your concerns, overpowering your mate for some time.

'Growing up' means you need to strike a balance---you can't overpower others, but you don't need to be silent. You must learn to speak at the right time and in the right way. This is as much an art as it is a science.

Remember what I said about your Protective Self attempting to speak for you, but in a harsh and hurtful manner towards the person you feel hurt by. The skill you must develop, then, is to speak up for yourself in a way that is respectful of others as well as yourself.

What might this look like and how might this sound? Let's review a situation with Jake.

"In the past, I would bully my wife when I disagreed with her. Now I'm learning to listen to her, honor her point of view, and then respectfully share my thoughts. It's not easy, but I've noticed that when I really listen to her, she is more interested in what I have to say."

Exactly! That's how it works. When we are respectful and curious about others, when they know we care about them, they will more likely care about us.

I'm reminded of the old adage that goes, "People don't care how much we know until they know how much we care."

Living With Integrity

Exposing and overcoming our shadow, Protective Self, means learning to live with integrity. *Integrity* comes from the word *integer,* meaning "at one." It means living consistently.

Living with integrity is a very difficult process. It means going to a lot of work to expose, understand, and transform our Protective Self. It means courageously learning about our shadowy parts and bringing them into the light where they can be healed and transformed.

Living with integrity also means living with humility and, to a certain extent, being comfortable with healthy shame. Healthy shame or remorse is the feeling of regret over actions taken and not taken. It means coming to terms with our hidden shadow parts and the damage they have done and continue to do. We courageously talk about the harm we are capable of doing when threatened. We learn to respect the power of our Protective Self.

Integrity for me means living openly and honestly. I don't shrink away from owning the harm I'm capable of doing. I am consistent. No duality. No Dr. Jekyll/ Mr. Hyde. Just one person.

Moving Ahead with Authenticity and Transparency

Thankfully it is possible to heal your disintegrated, protective parts. It is possible to fully own and transform your Protective Self, but that process—treatment—means living with authenticity and transparency.

Living with authenticity and transparency means living mindfully in every situation. It means monitoring your reactions and pausing to do RAIN whenever you feel threatened. Openness, honesty, and transparency heal.

As simple as this might sound, it's hard work. Most of us believe we live openly and transparently when nothing could be further from the truth. Many call a Bible Study an act of accountability and openness when it is often an act of image management—attempting to 'look good.'

It's hard to stand up and ask for our bad behavior to be called out. It is human nature, as we heard from the Apostle Paul, to have blind spots and self-defeating actions and attitudes. So, it will be critical that you cultivate a group of people who will really challenge you, who will ask you tough questions and insist on honest answers.

This means that you will routinely talk about the places and times you were triggered, your actions on your worst day, and the times your Protective Self came out. It won't be any fun to talk about such times, but you must make this a standard part of your week.

Do you have a place or friend/ accountability partner who will challenge you, who won't accept the glossy, neat, and tidy rendition of your story? Do you have a person who has the guts to call BS? If not, get to work. Find such a group and such a person.

Your life and recovery depend on it.

The Path Forward

Are you ready to live with integrity? Are you ready to fully own your shadow, Protective Self? If so, you have taken a huge step forward. Healing and denial cannot coexist. Honesty and transparency can't exist with self-protection and denial.

If you are part of a therapy group or have sought the help of a therapist, be honest. In the quiet of your own heart express what is alive and unwell. Move forward on ownership and healing. Then you will be more able to step back and observe what is taking place when angered or hurt, able to more thoughtfully choose a healthy path forward.

The Ripple Effect of Narcissism and Emotional Abuse

Chapter Seven: Dr. John Hudson

Over the years I have worked with many Narcissists and Emotional Abusers. As I consider the narcissistic traits and emotionally abusive behaviors, one story in particular comes to mind above all the others. It's about Jim and Linda.

There was a time in their struggling marriage when Jim stonewalled Linda for SEVEN months! He did not say a word to her for seven months. It would be easy to assume in this story that they were separated, but no. Not only did they still live together, but they were still sleeping in the same bed!

Linda shared how Jim would come home from work and greet the kids cheerfully and pet the dog; but would not utter a word in her direction. I can't imagine not talking to my wife for more than a day. How Jim did this, I still cannot fathom. As they shared this, it became very clear why Linda was hurting so badly.

Throughout the lifespan of any relationship, many things will occur, producing both good and bad experiences. When one behavior or attitude is directly connected to another result or outcome, we can see the result or outcome is a ripple effect. Not unlike tossing a stone into a pool and watching the ripples of water expand outward. It illustrates how small actions can lead to broader consequences.

The ripple effect illustrates the interconnectedness of actions and outcomes. It is a perfect illustration of how even a very minor event can set off a chain of reactions influencing a larger event.

Ripple effects are inevitable in every relationship. Do you remember a mentor or teacher in school with great fondness? Is this because he or she inspired you so positively you were motivated to pursue the career you are serving now? The pebble they dropped into the water (the motivation they inspired in you) would create the ripple effect of your career choice.

Think about when you were growing up. Think about the experiences you've had and the impact they've had on you over the course of your life. Most of us can associate happy times with good outcomes today.

However, when we think of times that were not so good, even times that were difficult or hard, we don't necessarily connect those to the attitudes and behaviors we experience today. The truth is, as mentioned in an earlier chapter, we were often in denial about the impact of what our past has done to our present and our future.

This is especially true when our past is full of negative experiences.

When a couple gets married, there's usually a logical, expected level of happiness accompanying their wedding day. This is a great example of a positive ripple effect in a marriage. However, if the wedding day is a disaster because of something the bride or groom did, the resulting ripple effect could be that trust is undermined from that day forward. If not corrected, the lasting ripple effect will affect the marriage negatively. Typically, in our encounters with couples through our work at the Marriage Recovery Center, we encounter negative ripple effects.

Ripple effects are those things that happen or come into existence because of an initial action/inaction or behavior.

Sometimes, the ripple effects of any behavior or attitude are hard to identify. It's even more difficult to directly connect these effects (or impacts) to past behaviors and past attitudes when the unhealthy actions that generated the negative ripple effects occurred years before.

You have the opportunity to produce positive or negative ripple effects. Which have you generated in your marriage? If you are reading this book because your wife has called you a Narcissist and/or an Emotional Abuser, you have created negative ripple effects by your actions or attitudes. In so many words, she has probably told you this. Can you see the connection?

There are many short-, mid-, and long-term effects of narcissism and emotional abuse. As a reminder, narcissistic abuse is a type of emotional abuse where you, the abuser, truly only care about yourself. And as you only care about yourself you use words and actions to control and manipulate your spouse's behavior and emotional state. Can you see it now?

The truth is your wife has been impacted throughout the course of your relationship. The length of time a spouse experiences several types of abuse, directly impacts whether they have mild effects or severe. Some spouses, maybe even yours, have suffered so much abuse for so long that they have sustained lifelong damage. Your spouse may never recover. No matter the hope you had for your marriage, it may end because of your abuse.

Although not the focus of this book, it is important to note the distinct long-term effects of individuals who were subjected to narcissism and emotional abuse as children. Adult children of narcissistic and emotionally abusive parents suffer in different ways than their spouses.

Put simply, child victims can carry this suffering over into their adult lives. With proper care, these adult children have a good chance of overcoming their past abusive experiences. If, however, your wife is one of these adult children, there is a significantly higher likelihood, that she will suffer greatly from your abusive behavior.

In the following pages, I will outline several types of "side effects" resulting from narcissistic and emotional abuse. Although these side effects differ in the degree of severity, they all cause harm to the abused. Keep in mind, you are not getting off because you only think you only abuse your spouse a little, or occasionally. Regardless of the severity of the abuse, the behaviors and attitudes associated with the abuse must all be addressed and corrected.

Other things to consider when trying to understand the ripple effect of narcissistic and emotional abuse are the frequency of when the abuse occurs and the age of the person on the receiving end of that abuse.

Narcissistic and emotional abuse has a huge impact on a person's self-esteem. The ongoing assault of manipulation, criticism, and demeaning attitudes gradually wears down the victim's sense of self-worth. Using these control tactics will destroy your spouse.

Has this happened in your relationship? Have things become so destructive that your wife ducks and hides when you come around? Why do you think you have this impact on her? Is it because you have figuratively beaten her down with your words to the point that she has no faith in herself or her abilities?

How many times has your wife exclaimed "I don't feel safe around you"? If you could imagine yourself in her position, enduring years of verbal abuse would you feel safe?

If manipulation has existed in your marriage over a long period of time, your wife may not even see what's going on. It's quite possible that early in your relationship, she could see or feel that something was wrong. Unfortunately, though, as your behavior persisted over time, she gave up, resigning herself to living a life of struggle. She felt she was no longer significant. At this point, your wife lost herself. Your actions forced her to become a shell of herself and merely an extension of you.

It is also because of this abuse that your wife may feel no self-worth and, in fact, would not even recognize the person she was before she met you. Because of this low self-worth, she may feel like she will never be good enough. To this end, your wife has given up on being an individual -- being her own person -- and having her own voice. Eventually, these feelings and experiences develop into worthlessness.

It is well documented that many spouses who have experienced narcissistic or emotional abuse develop depression. After months, or even years, of being told how dumb and useless they are, they begin to believe it. The despair this produces leaves your spouse believing she is worthless. Depression takes hold as a result of the accusations she now believes to be true.

The chaos you create as an abuser creates confusion and anxiety. Your efforts to rewrite or change history – through pushing your agenda – have caused your wife to question her reality. Because you have changed the narrative so often and for so long, your wife is confused.

What she once thought and believed to be reality does not seem true anymore because you've taken every opportunity to question her reality. You've repeatedly challenged her interpretation and perspective of what life is like with you, to the extent she now believes whatever you say to be true.

You've used blame-shifting to turn the trouble back on her.

She has become so confused she begins to believe your narrative and your interpretation of reality. Finally, she lacks her own version of your narrative. The only version of your marriage story left for her is the one you have forced on her. Let's review the impact of various emotionally abusive tactics on the abused.

Powering Over

The act of using emotional force to overwhelm and ultimately force your will on your spouse. The resulting ripple effect is your wife becomes so beaten down, that she eventually gives up, and gives in to not having a voice anymore.

Scapegoating

By placing the burden of responsibility on your spouse while projecting yourself in a positive light, you gradually paint your wife as the "bad mate". Eventually, she becomes so frustrated with being portrayed in this negative manner, she is unable to protect herself. Anytime you accuse your wife as the source of all the problems you're encountering in your marriage, you've slipped into scapegoating. Have you done this? Whether you do this intentionally or not, the effect is the same. Scapegoating ends in your spouse feeling 'run over' and this will destroy her trust in you.

Blame Shifting

Although somewhat like scapegoating, the distinction of this trait is the nuance of when you turn her words back on her. "You do it too." You may have heard this called tit-for-tat, calling out that the other does the same does not make it even. The resulting ripple effect is feeling overwhelmed with blame, especially if you've projected blame onto your wife to others outside of your marriage.

Ultimately, your wife becomes so overwhelmed with your blaming that she starts to question whether she might be to blame. If you blame shift long and often enough, your wife – because of the confusion you're creating – gets to a place where she doesn't trust her own memories of events.

Rage Reactions

Exploding in angry outbursts aimed at your spouse. This can produce so much fear that your wife does not feel safe with you or even in the relationship. Unhealthy anger explosions are extremely destructive. Angry rage is often a reaction to your "perceived" injury or injustice.

Where is this perceived injury coming from? Is your wife the true target of your angry outburst? A question to consider in this situation is, what experience is causing you so much pain that you are lashing out at those closest to you? Even if you are in a frustrating situation, raging behavior is not excusable. As anger is a secondary emotion, it's very important to discover what the source of your anger is.

Stonewalling

Retreating into silence with the intention of pushing your spouse away and isolating her. Ignoring your spouse is often more painful than any other emotionally abusive tactic. Stonewalling is the equivalent of being put in isolation. Stonewalling is also a form of neglect. A person left unattended is a person left unloved. Your wife does not want to be isolated or ignored. In fact, she needs to be heard – the opposite of being ignored.

Rewriting History

Pretending that you haven't committed a harmful action even to the point of presenting a completely different version of the past to cover it up. This action calls into question the very memories of your victim. The purposeful lies are intended to confuse your spouse and present a history you want to believe (and you want them to believe) even though you know it isn't true. Allowing the truth your wife knows as real to persist becomes unacceptable because the true story may cast you in a negative light.

The ripple effect resulting from this is confusion and chaos and creates a severe lack of trust.

Deception or Denial

Lying about, or denying an action or attitude existed to avoid any consequences. Clearly, the resulting ripple effect is the destruction of trust.

Gaslighting

Excuses and justifications are projected from one spouse to another to deflect any responsibility for harmful behavior. Of all the behaviors discussed, this is often the most harmful, because of the multiple destructive effects. Gaslighting alone is such "crazymaking" that your wife's head and heart are spinning. In addition to the ripple effects of anxiety, depression, and Post-Traumatic Stress Disorder (PTSD) – gaslighting has been linked to insomnia, weight gain or loss, memory loss, social isolation, and substance abuse. It's overwhelming to understand how one person can treat another so poorly that they suffer so greatly.

It is easy to see the abuse within your marriage has led to trust issues. Your wife, as your victim, has difficulty trusting you (and even others). She feels unsure about herself, making it nearly impossible to establish healthy boundaries for healthy living.

Because of these overwhelming trust issues, there may come a time when your wife questions everything and everyone around her (maybe it's already here) Can you see that she struggles to trust you and even others associated with you?

The trust issues could become so severe that she eventually believes you are going to leave her or betray her. She certainly may have already reached a point where she does not trust you. It may be impossible for her to believe you're ever being truthful, or that you're ever sincere, or that you don't have ulterior motives. Eventually, she may reach a stage where she is not even able to trust herself.

To keep peace or calm, your wife might cover for you with excuses or become overly protective to get approval from you. As a result of years of abuse, she may adopt some characteristics of codependence.

Codependency is a behavioral pattern that often arises in relationships where one person consistently prioritizes the needs of others over their own. Here are some common signs of codependency – some of which were mentioned earlier.

Low Self-Esteem

Codependent individuals tend to have low self-worth and struggle with self-image. Low self-esteem affects us in one of two ways. We constantly seek affirmation from everyone around us (especially our spouse) and this becomes overwhelming, or we are so self-defeating that no amount of affirmation lifts us out of a self-imposed state of depression. Either way, those around us feel like they can never support us enough.

Difficulty Identifying Emotions

They find it challenging to recognize, express, and communicate their own feelings and needs. Chaos results! As hard as you might try, you cannot accurately explain to your wife how you feel; much less clearly understand how she feels.

Self-Sacrifice

Codependents often put others' needs ahead of their own, oftentimes to their own detriment. This continuous state of giving up and giving in depletes even the strongest people.

Exaggerated Sense of Responsibility

They feel an intense loyalty and responsibility for the actions and emotions of others. This person becomes the savior for everyone around them. In a marriage, taking responsibility for the state of everything should be shared. However, the codependent is compelled (by herself or pressed by you -- her husband) to constantly TAKE charge of and responsibility for all the negative in your lives.

Confusing Love and Pity

Codependents may blur the lines between love and pity, often trying to rescue or be rescued by others. In efforts to care for you, your wife (through care and loving intent) ends up a victim of your pity parties. You "play the victim" and she slips into the role of having pity instead of loving you with truthful challenges to your victim mentality.

Fear of Abandonment

There's a persistent fear of rejection, abandonment, or anger from others. When fear exists, many of us react in unhealthy ways. You or your wife are likely to report feelings of uncertainty about your future together and even threaten to leave or stonewall to the point of creating isolation.

Compromising Values

They compromise their own values, interests, and integrity to please others or avoid conflict.

High Sensitivity to Others' Feelings

Codependents are acutely attuned to the emotions of others and may take on those feelings. As you can see, all these traits resulting from codependency can have a negative impact on your wife and your relationship. In the context of your marriage, any of these traits may be compounded by the daily stresses of life.

When multiple traits exist, the impact on your wife is even more severe. If each one of these traits weighed 10 pounds, alone it wouldn't be a burden. However, what if (and this is likely) more than one trait – even 4-5 – exist at the same time, the burden is overwhelming, even crushing.

When your wife is exposed to Narcissistic or Emotional Abuse long enough, there's a high chance she will begin to experience physical symptoms. She may struggle with headaches, physical pains, high blood pressure, and stomach issues. In addition, it's not uncommon for people suffering from various types of emotional abuse to develop cognitive issues. These issues can eventually lead to an inability to think clearly or concentrate on even the most mundane tasks.

As you begin to recognize the unhealthy parts of your past and the actions and attitudes you've exhibited, your opportunity is to accept the ripple effects and the resulting impact on your wife. No more denial! Your wife is hurting. You are probably hurting, too. It's time to allow the healthy shame addressed earlier in the book to settle in and drive you toward positive change.

You can be healthy! Seize the opportunity – don't let another day go by. There's a lot of hard work ahead and it is going to take a long time to recover. The alternative is that your wife continues to suffer. What are the potential outcomes? In the next section, you will be presented with ideas of what to do, and how to prioritize changes and become a much healthier version of you.

What Does a Healthy Man Look Like Anyway?

Chapter Eight: Dr. David B. Hawkins

You've been challenged, repeatedly hearing 'Don't do this,' 'Stop doing that,' 'Change.' It's overwhelming, right? You've been living your life, your way, for a long, long time, so to simply stop being, well you, is far easier said than done. Changing is difficult.

You have undoubtedly attempted change. You've had fits and starts, successes and failures. You've tried and failed, tried again and failed again. You've probably found this new life of treatment and recovery is like navigating a minefield, never knowing when or where you might step on an explosive, and it feels devastating when that occurs.

I doubt you are intentionally causing harm, of course, but are you putting your heart and soul into becoming a healthy man? At this point are you even clear about what a healthy man looks like? Most men aren't sure what they're aiming for, and so it is not surprising they usually miss the mark.

The goals for men are often unclear, which makes the task even more daunting. To be told to 'Grow up' is vague. 'Change' is equally vague. 'Figure it out' is an insistent message that leaves you even more angry and confused.

We want to be clear about what is expected of you. We want to ensure that you have clear goals and a clear target, so you have no excuses for making healthy changes. That's what this chapter is about.

Lost and Disoriented

Let's consider the notion of being lost. When you're lost, to one extent or another you're also disoriented. You've lost your bearings and are uncertain about how to proceed.

I remember a time several years ago when I took my wife sailing, we needed to move our boat from one harbor to another. She was not thrilled about spending a cold day in a 20-foot sailboat with me as the captain, but I assured her I knew what I was doing.

(I didn't!)

We left the marina very early on a chilly, November morning. With my calculations, we would reach our destination by late afternoon. Shortly after leaving the harbor a cold wind began to blow, and the temperatures dropped dramatically hinting of snow. My confidence diminished as the weather changed, but I told Christie, everything was under control. It was not.

I sailed on. I was in over my head but didn't want to show my fears and doubts to my wife. I didn't want to admit this was all a terrible mistake.

I began to panic. The navigation was far more difficult than I anticipated, and the evening was setting in. With each hour the weather worsened, and my fears grew. Not wanting to frighten my wife, I frantically looked for navigational signs, but again, this was all way beyond my skills.

By now Christie could sense I was lost amidst numerous islands, none of which had directional signs.

The wind was too strong for my sailing skills, so we motored slowly on and as evening set in, I was concerned we were running low on fuel. I had to fess up that we were lost and running low on fuel.

By an incredible stroke of luck, we bumped into a mooring buoy, where we tied up and spent a very cold and uncomfortable night. Even lower in confidence, and feeling humiliated, I arose at dawn and was able to navigate to our destination by mid-morning.

Christie could not get off the boat fast enough

Many of the men I've counseled are as bull-headed as I was that day. They are too proud to change course, determined to stick to the path they are on, yet uncertain about their direction at the same time. How is this possible?

The answer again comes down to a stubbornness and reluctance to admit being wrong. It's hard to admit being lost, and stubborn pride stops you from reaching out for help.

Add to your stubborn pride the fact there are some areas of your life working okay. These okay parts give you ammunition to use when you're feeling insecure. However, let's be honest. Most men know what they're doing is not bringing the relationship satisfaction, but they don't feel in enough distress to wave the white flag of defeat or cry out for help. Subsequently, they remain lost and disoriented.

Desperately Needing Direction

So, what's the answer to this dilemma? It lies in cultivating an attitude of receptivity, humility, and openness to new directions. It means crying out, "I'm lost. Will someone help me?" Then it means looking for the best help possible.

Every man must come to the place where they admit to being lost. Whenever someone admits to the severity of being lost, being truly unable to find their way, then and only then will the lost person be receptive to being helped. That is when the lost man is ready to seek the counsel of a wiser person, someone they deem to have the attributes they aspire to. It involves believing and saying,

"I'm lost. Will you help me?"

More than that, when you are honestly ready to change, you will honestly seek counsel. You will eagerly seek help. You will admit to hurting your wife and cry out and find counseling for your specific situation.

Finding counsel will be a fantastic beginning, a starting place to begin the work towards needed change. From this space you let go of what you know, the path you've chosen and clung to in the past and begin seeking new information.

She Doesn't Know Either

You may be tempted to ask your mate to map out directions for you, but I have sobering news for you. It's likely she doesn't know what you need either. Oh, she knows what must change, but she can't instruct you on how to do it. Realistically, it's not her job and she is likely sick and tired of providing direction and pushing you to change. It's your job to find the right help and to go about making changes. It's your job to turn away from her and seek expert help---someone who knows about narcissism and emotional abuse.

Likely your mate is ready to say, "I'm done doing all the work. This one is all yours. You pick up the ball and run with it for a change." She has likely pleaded with you to get specific help for some time. Most spouses of narcissistic men have been 'over functioning' for a long time and are weary. It's on you now to give up emotional laziness and seek help.

It's true. She has been working too hard for change and is more than ready for you to take leadership on these issues. She wants you to watch videos, go to counseling, talk to someone more mature than yourself. She's right. It is time for you to take initiative, determine a new direction and discover ways to become a healthy man.

Many Experts Don't Know

It seems harsh to hear that your spouse is tired and now it's all on you, but guess what? I have more bad news. Not only does your mate not know how to bring about the changes you need, but many professionals are also in the dark when it comes to narcissism and emotional abuse. Most have read a book or two, taken meager training and have counseled a few folks with narcissistic and emotionally abusive traits, and so only have a superficial understanding of the problem.

What does this mean for you? It means you need to search to find the best help you can, help that is very familiar with the treatment of narcissism and emotional abuse. Becoming a healthy man means entrusting yourself to an expert on these issues, someone who will challenge you about being lost and still stubbornly clinging to old ways. You must admit your lost, facing the fact that clinging to old ways of functioning keeps you stuck. Only by admitting these traits can you learn all you need to learn about becoming an emotionally healthy man.

Emotional Maturation

Again, remember that becoming healthy is not only about letting go of old ways and giving up emotionally abusive patterns.

It's also about embracing new ways of functioning.

Since narcissistic and emotional abuse is largely about emotional immaturity, any reading and studying you do on that topic is a good starting point for cultivating emotional maturity.

As you begin exploring the topic of emotional maturation, you might assume since you've reached a certain chronological age, you've arrived emotionally. You'd be wrong. Chronological maturity has nothing to do with emotional maturity.

In a recent group therapy session, Jake, who had by now grown in his personal development, shared the following story:

"I'm beginning to think I've got the maturity of a little boy when it comes to my marriage. I can see that I react very childishly with my wife and that's been pretty hard to see and admit. When my wife asks me to do something I don't want to do, I either refuse to do it or say I'm going to do it and then conveniently forget. Then, when she reminds me, I accuse her of nagging. She gets mad and I criticize her for getting angry. I'm beginning to see just how childish I am."

Others in the group nodded in appreciation and understanding, many of whom were in the same boat. Jake was encouraged to continue in understanding and to grow emotionally.

Jake has made a lot of progress and is on the right path.

Admitting these patterns is the beginning opportunity for change. He's beginning to see his emotional immaturity and the 'craziness' his emotional immaturity brings to the marriage. Can you see how emotional immaturity leads to emotional abuse? It's critical to review all your actions through this lens.

The following are *10 signs of emotional maturity* you can review as a starting point for learning about this issue:

1. *Healthy men cultivate emotional resilience and regulation.* Healthy people learn to manage their emotions and share them effectively with their mate—not so with the narcissistically and emotionally abusive man. He often has little resilience and is easily offended. Relationships are challenging and differences can be places of friction and so challenges must be expected and met with emotional balance.

2. *Healthy men take ownership of problems and makes repair for harm done.*
   Healthy people take ownership for their part in problems. When
   they've made a mistake, they quickly own it and offer reparations—
   not so with the narcissistically and emotionally abusive man. He
   takes no ownership of problems. He rarely sees himself as the one
   owing an apology.

3. *Healthy men share with compassion and empathy.* Healthy people are
   compassionate toward each other, showing empathy and ongoing
   concern for their mate—not so with the narcissistically and
   emotionally abusive man—he has little empathy and is too self-
   centered to be compassionately connected to his mate.

4. *Healthy men have simple and effective interactions.* Healthy people
   understand that interactions should be easy, simple and effective.
   Issues are resolved quickly. Healthy men know conflict must be
   limited and joyful, humorous interactions must prevail---
   emotionally abusive men engage in debate, argument, opposition.
   Every significant interaction is a challenge, which is exhausting for
   his mate.

5. *Healthy men practice effective problem-solving.* Healthy people are able to
   step back and view a problem objectively. They don't shame or
   blame one another, but tackle problems effectively—the

narcissistically and emotionally abusive man doesn't know how to effectively problem-solve.

6. *Healthy men give and receive love.* Healthy people give and receive love. They are intentional about showing each other, in small and large ways, that they care. They are able to extend themselves for the welfare of others and acknowledge what they need to be loved well. The narcissistically and emotionally abusive man cannot give mature love.

7. *Healthy men cultivate clarity of thinking.* Healthy people seek to think clearly, free from 'thinking errors' that erode trust, magnify problems and shame one another. Clear thinking leads to solving problems and moving on with enjoying relationships—the narcissistically and emotionally abusive man displays 'thinking errors' including entitlement, deferring problem-solving, minimization, excuse-making.

8. *Healthy men practice healthy self-care.* Healthy people know they must keep their minds and bodies healthy, and it is their responsibility to do so. Subsequently, they consider how nutrition, exercise, as well as mind/ body and spiritual practices help them—the narcissistically and emotionally abusive man doesn't know how to care for himself well.

9. *Healthy men reinforce healthy boundaries.* Healthy people are mindful of where they end, and their mate begins. They consider 'whose business is whose business,' not telling the other what they 'should' do, think or be. They manage and reinforce their personal boundaries and respect the boundaries of others---the narcissistically and emotionally abusive man has no healthy boundaries, believing he has the right to control others.

10. *Healthy men practice acceptance of others.* Finally, healthy people understand the individuality of their mate and appreciate differences. While they may ask for changes, they understand they cannot manipulate or coerce the other into changing—the narcissistically and emotionally abusive man lacks acceptance of others.

This list may feel overwhelming, but emotional maturity is a big deal. It is a critically important issue for living in a healthy relationship. Using these ten signs of emotional maturity as a measuring stick, how do you rate? A better question might be, how might your mate score you?

Time to 'Grow Up'

It's time to 'grow up.' Again, this is all easier said than done. What do I mean when I say, 'grow up?' Growing up is often characterized as the ability to process and cope effectively and responsibly with your emotions, as well as the thoughts and actions of others.

This definition of 'growing up' should become your yardstick. Am I paying close attention to my feelings and am I making good choices based upon those feelings? If your mate says something and you feel hurt, do you take time to process those feelings? If not, your passivity may very well lead to passive aggression, stonewalling, or sarcastic comments.

Growing up means you are not dependent upon others to act in any certain way for your happiness. You must not rely on others to act, think or conduct themselves in any way to help you be the person you intend to be. You must be able to regulate yourself no matter how others act around you.

If you say to yourself, "If it wasn't for her........., I'd be fine," you're on the wrong path. If you expect others to change so that you'll feel better, your blaming others for your moods and actions. This must change. You must be the source and focus of your own well-being.

Imagine you have an internal thermostat. No matter what the temperature is on the outside, you're able to regulate yourself internally. You can make good choices to be emotionally sober, balanced and have a clear direction for your life.

In one of my early graduate courses in psychology, we learned about the concept of *'internal locus of control.'* If I'm in charge of my life, determining my life direction and choices, I have an 'internal locus of control.' If, however, I'm directed by others, unduly influenced by others and allow others to control me, then I have an 'external locus of control.'

Another way to think about this is if I'm filled with resentment, expecting someone to change so I can be happy, I have an external locus of control and need to rethink my expectations.

Growing up means I take full responsibility for my wellbeing. I make good choices so that I am free from pouting, blaming, angry outbursts. I am able to maintain emotional stability and make any necessary changes so that I have control over my life.

Emotional Sobriety

Another lens through which to view your progress and a measure of whether you are growing up or not, involves the topic of emotional sobriety. Central to the issue of becoming a healthy man is the concept of *'emotional sobriety.'*

What do I mean by 'emotional sobriety?' Emotional sobriety is emotional steadiness, emotional balance. This emotional steadiness comes when we accept life on life's terms, accepting people for who they are, accepting situations for how they come to us. When we expect people to be different than who they are, or fuss about circumstances not being what we want them to be, we are emotionally intoxicated and unbalanced. We think and act irrationally. We are moody, uncentered and perhaps even unwell.

Bill Wilson, from Alcoholics Anonymous, shared his thoughts on 'emotional sobriety':

"Those adolescent urges that so many of us have for top approval, perfect security, and perfect romance -- urges quite appropriate to age seventeen -- prove to be an impossible way of life when we are at age forty-seven or fifty-seven. Since AA began, I've taken immense wallops in all these areas because of my failure to grow up, emotionally and spiritually. My God, how painful it is to keep demanding the impossible, and how very painful to discover finally, that all along we have had the cart before the horse."

Wilson's thoughts highlight the importance of managing our expectations and accepting people for who they are.

Acceptance is the hallmark of emotional maturity and becoming a healthy man.

Coming Out of Isolation

Growing up is impossible to do alone. Yet, as necessary as it is to connect and surround yourself with men who will encourage and challenge you, most men choose to go it alone---to their detriment.

I think Henry David Thoreau had it right when he said,

"The mass of men lead lives of quiet desperation."

When I ask men how many good friends they have, the answer is the same—few. When I ask men if they have someone they could call when feeling down, they answer the same—maybe.

What is going on here? Are men still caught up in being too proud to admit needing others? I think so. You need to be part of a caring and accountable community. You cannot do this work alone. We all need people and a group we can turn to, to sort out the complexities of our lives.

Most men feel completely alone, so don't feel bad if no one comes to mind when I ask if you have anyone to reach out to. It's common. Men often navigate life alone, and that's part of the problem. Men need one another, as much as women need one another.

No More Emotional Laziness

Another critical step in becoming emotionally mature, in addition to giving up isolation, is giving up emotional laziness and taking initiative. Whether or not you have a 'real life mentor' whom you believe has qualities of emotional immaturity or not, it's still your responsibility to find your way. I'm challenging you, again, to muster up incredible resolve, initiative, to use all that you're going through as an opportunity to change and grow.

Taking initiative means giving up laziness and fiercely pursuing healing. You may need to scratch and dig, searching high and low for support groups, videos, books, and anything that can give you direction. You will need to become active, ridding yourself of any passivity. No great leader is going to jump out of the woodwork and save the day for you. You must save your own day.

Countless times I've run into men who were unwilling to really dig deep and go after healing. Countless times I've run into men who remained stuck in 'cluelessness,' hoping their mate, their pastor, their therapist, anyone would save the day for them. This is called magical thinking, and it is still a horrendous 'thinking error.'

E-Motions

We could not possibly talk about emotional maturity without talking about emotions, the foundation for connection to yourself and others. Another aspect of emotional maturity means listening to, and understanding, your emotions.

Emotions have been called "energy in motion." Think about it. Emotions guide us, direct us, and at times may even control us. Emotions are trailheads that lead us to the work we must do.

Recently a man in the group made an accusation that I've heard before.

"Dr. Hawkins," he said. "It seems to me that you see every man as the culprit and every woman as the victim. You've made a business out of it. I don't think it's fair."

"Tell me more about what you're feeling," I said.

"I think you're making a business out of your work," he continued.

"Well," I said, "to a certain extent that's true. This is my life's work. But I want to know more about what you're feeling." "I just told you," he said.

"No, you told me your thoughts," I said. "You actually made a judgment. I'm curious about your feelings. Can anyone else in group help?"

"Maybe distrust," another man said.

"Threatened," another said.

"That's what I would guess," I said. "And bear in mind that whatever it is we're feeling is probably not the first time we've felt it. Furthermore, our feelings are often influenced by our past and so we can learn about ourselves from our immediate experience." I paused and then asked the first man a question.

"Do you feel distrust of me? Perhaps threatened? Have you experienced those feelings with others in your life?"

"Sure," he said. "That's been a big deal in my past."

"Then this experience, what you're feeling right now, can be a chance to 'grow up.' You have an opportunity to learn more about yourself, listen to your feelings, and make healthy choices. I'm here to help you, but remember, your mate may not be. It's best to do that work here and now."

This man had experienced what has been called a 'Trailhead,' an opportunity to learn more about himself. He was on the verge of discovering that his immediate reaction to me was influenced by his past and he had some healing work to do.

This healing work requires diligence, focus and a huge desire to grow up and become healthy. Armed with this motivation, however, great things can occur.

You Have the Direction You Need

Though you undoubtedly feel alone and bewildered, I want to remind you of an important truth: *you have all the information you need to change and grow.* Now I know that sounds like a contradiction to what I've been saying. It's both true that you need others, and you have received a ton of information to begin your healing journey.

Consider this: you have a lifetime of experiences to draw upon to help you determine how to move forward with your life. When you give up laziness and reflect on all the feedback from your mate you've already been given, and really set out to become a healthy man, you can find your way.

There is a great saying: "When the student is ready, the teacher appears." Are you ready for a teacher? Open your eyes and look around. Do you see anyone who might take this journey with you?

Again, I know this sounds like a contradiction because of what I've been saying about needing others, and especially needing to listen to wise counsel. For as lost as you might be, and as disoriented as you might feel, you have the capacity to be courageous, confident and clear. With God's help, we have an inexhaustible source of wisdom available to us. If we pause, reflect and deeply consider what others are saying to us, we can establish a new, healthy direction for our lives.

Scripture tells us to pursue wisdom, that it is available to all of us. "If you need wisdom, ask our generous God, and he will give it to you." (James 1: 5) It remains your responsibility to change!

Take a moment and jot down what you believe to be a *Good Orderly Direction (GOD)* for your life. Collect your thoughts. Reflect on your emotions. Have any truths emerged for you?

Iron Sharpens Iron

As I've said, this journey of growing up, of becoming a healthy man, is not a solo expedition. Far from it. You need other men who are intent as well on becoming healthy and you have a lot to offer others as well.

Solomon used the analogy, "iron sharpens iron." What did he mean? Iron, in Biblical times, contained varying amounts of impurities and was of different strengths. Sharpening a tool involved refining a sharp edge on a tool designed for cutting. Sharpening was done by grinding away material on the tool with another abrasive substance harder than the tool itself.

In other words, if you desire to be strengthened, you need to spend time with a person willing to challenge you to grow. You must invest yourself with others you want to model your life after. Who might that be? Do any men around you come to mind? Begin compiling a list of people who might support you on your journey.

Emotional Intelligence

One final principle for becoming a healthy man involves the importance of emotional intelligence. Narcissism and emotional abuse occur within the context of emotional ignorance. This is not about literal IQ, but rather one's ability to accurately read a situation and know how to respond to it.

Emotional intelligence refers to our capacity to recognize our feelings, the feelings of others around us, and choosing wisely how to respond to any challenge in that situation. This takes lots of practice, but with work, we all can become smarter emotionally.

We teach men in our Core group that they have the opportunity, in any given situation, to make matters better or worse. Since emotions are contagious, you will have many opportunities to de-escalate a situation or escalate it. You can deescalate matters by keeping your cool, empathizing with your mate and wisely problem-solving.

None of this is easy to do, but with practice, you can become more and more effective. You can be an emotional leader in your home. By maintaining your emotional sobriety, you positively impact everyone around you.

It has been said that resonance is contagious, and so is dissonance. In other words, keeping your cool will be contagious, just as surely as getting angry will increase the likelihood that others around you will get angry as well.

Aristotle said, "Anyone can become angry---that is easy. But to be angry with the right person, to the right degree, at the right time, for the right purpose, and in the right way—that is not easy." Well said.

Back On Track

Are you embracing the idea of becoming a healthy man? The more you embrace this healing journey, the clearer your path will become. You will grow in self-confidence and courage and know the right thing to do at any given moment. You will get a sense that you are 'back on track.'

Remember, every time you are emotionally shaken, every time you get angry, hurt, or defensive, is an opportunity to step back, reflect, understand, and get back on track.

Vulnerability as a Path to Connection

Chapter Nine: Dr. John Hudson

How can vulnerability ever be a strength? Isn't this a sign of weakness? A decade ago, nobody talked about emotional vulnerability. Being vulnerable emotionally was generally compared to being weak, or at least with being easily hurt or frightened. Did anyone say to you as you were growing up, "Don't show any weakness"; "Be strong"; or "Crying is for sissies"? Of course, this notion is absurd. If you were told such things growing up, you were told a lie.

I met Jeff and Linda through a request for marriage counseling. Jeff was a rugged man who appeared to have no emotions; he was stone-faced. You could tell by the way he walked into our session he didn't want to meet with me. His wife had demanded it. No matter my questions, Jeff ignored me. while Linda was a flurry of words and seemed amazingly hopeful. It was obvious by his silence; Jeff didn't want to engage. Even when Linda freely showed her frustrations, Jeff remained stoic.

"Jeff, are you sensing Linda's anger?" I asked. You guessed it, no response. It was as if Jeff couldn't feel anything.

At this point, I changed course and invited Jeff to tell me about his work. Suddenly, Jeff came to life as he told me about his law practice. As a litigating attorney of nearly 30 years, he was quite proud of his accomplishments.

Jeff shared how he started as an apprentice law clerk while still pursuing his law degree. Within five years after passing the bar, Jeff became a partner in the firm. In the courtroom and for his clients, he was ruthless. I asked him to explain his success, and Jeff said, "I never get emotionally involved".

It was then that I understood. What propelled Jeff to success in his role as a lawyer was destroying his marriage. Linda knew it, too. She had known it for a long time. No matter how many times or ways Linda tried to share this reality with Jeff, he couldn't understand.

Maybe Jeff was never willing to discuss anything with vulnerability because it didn't make sense to him? It is not a natural, daily, occurrence in the lives of many men, and frankly it is painful. If you've ever felt the nervousness of asking your boss for the promotion you rightly deserve but haven't been offered or saying "I love you" for the first time, you might know the feeling. It is awkward and anxiety-provoking.

You might be more familiar with the uncertainty of waiting for a phone call with test results from a doctor or reaching out to a friend who just lost a loved one. It's about as welcome as death or filing taxes. So why talk about it? Allowing ourselves to be emotionally vulnerable is a tremendous source of strength and the only way we can truly connect in our most personal relationships.

It is critical to fully understand what we're talking about here. There are two types of vulnerability – healthy and unhealthy vulnerability. In fact, at the Marriage Recovery Center, we are very familiar with what it means to be a vulnerable (covert) narcissist.

This is, clearly, an unhealthy version of vulnerability. Healthy vulnerability is sharing your life – your emotions and feelings -with your spouse. Are you hiding? Hiding your emotions, your true feelings and dreams?

What defines whether or not your vulnerability is healthy are your underlying motives. Vulnerability alone is not good or bad. However, intentions related to vulnerability matter. So, what are – or have been – your intentions? If you are using some level of unhealthy emotional defensive tactics to protect yourself from exposure – this is UNHEALTHY "vulnerability".

As a whole, if you intend to understand and care for your wife and marriage through opening up, the result can be a closer more intimate relationship. If, however, your intention – whether stated or not – was to use or hurt your wife, then clearly this vulnerability was a tool used to serve yourself. When

"vulnerability" is used as a selfish tool, it's abuse. This is not a healthy vulnerability.

So, what is healthy emotional vulnerability? Healthy emotional vulnerability is most often felt as anxiety (although, the good kind of anxiety) without being rejected, shamed, or judged as inadequate.

Think about this concept for a moment. Doubt is real. However, when we are rejected, shamed, or judged by someone close to us – someone we care about, this introduces doubt. We can struggle when these things exist, and even question ourselves. It is deeply tied to anxiety. In fact, very often those who suffer from chronic anxiety have particular difficulty accepting the uncertainty in their daily lives. This results in a tendency, then, to hold back our own ideas or even reject our ideas altogether.

For example, the risk of feeling rejected if the object of your love does not love you back or accept your perspective. Or, that your boss will not only deny the raise; but will also tell you why you are not worthy of it. When these instances of rejection happen long enough, the instigated anxiety becomes constant – there's no escape.

Emotional exposure: You've decided to partner with someone, and you begin to fear this person will get to know you better than you know yourself.

These situations are more frightening to some of us than to others, depending upon our personal histories, our cultural backgrounds, and our basic personality traits.

The feeling of shame is a particular risk for many individuals, especially if they were raised in a shame-based culture. However, nearly everyone struggles with emotional vulnerability to some degree every day. (The exceptions are those with no desire to feel connected, such as extreme narcissists and sociopaths.)

So – back to our original question in this chapter. *How can vulnerability be a strength?* It is through pushing ourselves to be vulnerable that we can understand, feel empathy, forgive each other, and know that we are worthy of love and belonging. For most men, this is unnatural. For a narcissistic man – it's impossible!

"Vulnerability is the birthplace of love, belonging, joy, courage, empathy, and creativity" —Dr. Brene Brown, 2012

Dr. Brown strikes a chord in me with her quote on vulnerability. It takes emotional courage to share our feelings with those who are important to us and to accept their feelings as valid and important. Being vulnerable allows us to create new ideas and to see fresh possibilities that were previously blocked from our minds. We take the risk that our creations will be judged poorly or rejected and that we may feel shame or inadequacy as a result.

However, we risk failure to have the chance of success.

How does vulnerability improve our close relationships? Generally speaking, emotional vulnerability is different for men than it is for women. More accurately, it differs for those who identify as male or female, largely due to social and cultural expectations of these genders. Women generally feel that they must "Do it all; do it perfectly, and never let them see you sweat!" Men tend to feel that they must follow the rule: "Do not be perceived as weak."

It is not the other men (teammates, coaches, etc.) in men's lives who reinforce this message as much as it is the women in their lives. What does this tell us about how male-female couples might improve their relationships? It requires a good amount of empathy to understand each other's sources of shame and to overcome our fear of being emotionally vulnerable.

She does not need him to solve her problems, but only for him to hear them and show caring. She wants to know that what she does, and who she is, "is enough" and worthy of being loved. He is not likely to talk about his feelings nor empathize with hers if he is not allowed to show his weakness. He wants to know that he is loved for who he is and that it is okay to feel afraid or uncertain.

The personal story of a colleague of mine is relevant here. I'm sharing this story with the hope of being helpful to female readers and the men whom they love. My colleague's twin brother was struck with a neuromuscular disease like Lou Gehrig's when he was still in college. He was told that he would gradually lose all muscular control, and so in effect become paralyzed over the next 6 to 8 years.

When I talked to my colleague further, I recall the fear in his expression when he talked about his brother's diagnosis, knowing that the illness would impact his ability to do even the simplest self-care routines. He would be facing the loss of his brother's health, independence, and his role as a future family provider. He had the courage to tell me he was afraid of what was to come. I was also afraid – for him. I was terrified.

I wish I had found the courage to share my fear with him at that moment. It might have made my reassurances more meaningful to him.

My lack of bravery, which would certainly have strengthened my friend, was lost. It was missing because I didn't, at that time, know how to embrace the value of vulnerability.

Embrace your own vulnerability and that of the people you love. Be open to sharing what you feel and taking those risks when your sense of judgment tells you that the risk is well worth it.

Being vulnerable in a relationship means taking a risk. There's a chance of getting hurt, but there's also an opportunity for connection and growth. Opening up to someone isn't always an easy thing to do. We may fear that if our spouse knows our biggest fears and secrets, they may think differently of us or even reject us.

Being vulnerable means risking getting hurt. It can be especially hard to open up to someone new if we've been hurt in the past when we handed someone our heart. But here's the thing: If we never let ourselves be vulnerable in our relationships, how can someone actually get to know us? How can those relationships get deeper? The short answer: They can't get to know us, and we won't have a deep relationship. Relationships need vulnerability — from both partners — to thrive.

What then, does vulnerability look like in a relationship? Vulnerability can take many different forms in a relationship because it means different things to different people. But in general, vulnerability in marriage means you remain open to sharing all parts of yourself with your wife and not being afraid of being judged and criticized.

We then understand the value of seeking to feel comfortable enough to turn towards our loved ones in our lowest moments rather than trying to isolate ourselves and turn away from their support. This can involve feeling comfortable enough to share your thoughts, beliefs, and values with your spouse. Feeling safe enough to tell them about your past and things that have happened to you indicates you are operating with healthy vulnerability.

The result – you can share your feelings — even when those feelings are difficult ones, like sadness, anger, or frustration — in a diplomatic way. Speaking the truth in love – sharing without judgment or condemnation!

If you're hurt by something your spouse does, focus on their actions, not them. Attacking your spouse, is not the problem, tears that person down. Responding vulnerably means speaking in terms of how their actions impacted you — such as saying, 'When you made that joke, I felt dismissed' — rather than attacking the other person by saying, 'You always make meanest jokes about me'.

Did you catch the difference? Being direct, and sharing your feelings or the impact on you, promotes the opportunity for your spouse to show empathy. If you condemn your spouse for what they said or assign motives that aren't true, you push her away.

Being vulnerable means accepting that you can't control what will happen as a result of sharing; but that you'll still act or speak in a way that's authentic to you. When we speak honestly (with vulnerability/transparency) from a place of how we feel, when we share our fears and dreams with another, we give somebody the power to either hear us or to hurt us. Even though this is risky, the connection is worth it!

Benefits of Vulnerability

As scary as being vulnerable may feel, it can also be incredibly beneficial. Vulnerability is the glue that draws individuals together instead of pushing them apart. Without this important glue, our relationship risks being shallow.

If we only share the comfortable and safe parts of ourselves, our relationships won't grow. The truth is a shallow relationship is one that barely survives. I've heard this quote – or something similar – a shallow grave rots the body. So, it is with a marriage – a shallow connection rots the marriage.

Vulnerability Deepens Your Bond

Vulnerability fosters closeness, trust, and intimacy because it tells the person you're with that you trust them. This allows you to truly get to know each other: how you think, what you value, and what you aspire to.

Vulnerability allows people to understand each other on a deeper level, even with their insecurities and their deepest feelings, which can lead to greater empathy in both partners. As you know, from earlier chapters, empathy is the path to connection in more intimate relationships.

Vulnerability Encourages Self-Regulation and Belonging

If we practice getting more comfortable with things that are typically uncomfortable, like asserting our needs or revealing insecurity, we're actually teaching ourselves how to regulate difficult feelings and cope with them.

Vulnerability Also Reduces Feelings of Shame

Being vulnerable can help us no longer feel weighed down by fear and shame, or whatever it is we're carrying. Our vulnerability is a way to foster connections, even when our shame may be telling us we don't deserve it.

This means that when we accept someone when they're vulnerable, we're telling them they're not alone and that they belong, despite their potential fears of not being worthy.

Vulnerability can help reduce conflict because vulnerability encourages open communication, intimacy, closeness, and self-regulation, it can ease tension and conflict. In healthy relationships, vulnerability paves the way for spouses to take accountability and inspires honest communication, rather than destructive behaviors such as deflecting, avoiding, or blaming the other person during a conflict. This helps lessen the chances of an argument escalating. You might even be able to disagree – without arguing?!

Tips For Building Vulnerability

Of course, if being vulnerable were easy, we'd all do it all the time. The truth is, it can be scary and difficult — and if things backfired in our past relationships, it could make it even harder to want to put ourselves out there again in the future. Despite it feeling scary, there are small things you can do to encourage vulnerability in your relationship to make it seem a little more manageable. Here are some tips:

Start slow - Start with sharing something small that you don't tell a lot of people. Then gauge your wife's response: Is she supportive? Or does she laugh or dismiss your vulnerability? If she does respond well, consider sharing again — maybe something a little bigger or scarier. If you have the courage to share, it is likely your wife will share in return.

Be honest - Give your genuine opinion, without altering it based on how you think your spouse might feel about it, or ask for what you really want, instead of what you think you 'should' want.

Express your needs - Our wives aren't mind-readers, and we must learn to tell each other what we need. If your spouse doesn't know what you need from them, it can be easy to feel like your needs aren't being met, which leads to greater resentment and frustration. However, you must also understand how critical it is to listen to her needs as well. In fact, learning to ASK her what she needs is imperative if you intend to prioritize her concerns over your own. If you don't, you will cause her to shut down, harming your relationship.

If your partner hurts you, let them know. When you feel hurt by your spouse, try not to react with anger. Instead, respond with a pause. Slow down your response when you feel hurt. When you can accurately identify your feeling(s) and what they did to hurt you, tell them — without accusatory words. Focus on making "I" statements, such as, "I feel hurt that you said that to me." Try to be as specific as possible. Language is our best means of expressing feeling understood and supported.

Model Vulnerability

You have the opportunity to lead in this area. How you lead in your life and actions/attitudes – your wife is likely to follow. If she doesn't … maybe you waited too long, and she can't trust your motives.

You can't force someone to be vulnerable with you, but you can model it for them, which might prompt them to respond in kind. The more you create safety and show vulnerability, the safer your partner may feel and become comfortable enough to share their emotional experience.

You can also reassure your partner that you're not going to betray them. This could be an underlying fear your wife has, especially if she has had destructive past relationship experiences with you. So, affirming your partner and giving her reassurance will help her learn that you are a safe person for her to be with and possibly open up to.

Ask Open-Ended Questions

Open-ended questions can encourage your spouse to be vulnerable. This type of question helps you receive the truth you need to better understand her. Of course, the key is to listen. Don't assume you already know the answer and understand their experience. For example, you could ask, "Why do you feel like that?" or "What was that like for you?" If she responds, give her your full, undivided attention, and believe her experience.

Acceptance goes a long way to building trust.

If You're Still Struggling with Vulnerability, Ask Yourself Why

"If you're struggling with opening up or being vulnerable with your wife, I challenge you to explore what's going on. Could it be you never experienced vulnerability? Was this never modeled for you while you were growing up? Did you have a negative emotional experience after being vulnerable in the past?

It can be helpful to talk openly about what it means to be vulnerable. This could be the perfect time to connect with a mental health professional. Understanding your own obstacles is often the first step in overcoming them.

Takeaway

Vulnerability is essential to a relationship. It can help foster closeness, intimacy, and trust. Without it, relationships tend to remain superficial — or partners can begin to feel disconnected and resentful of one another. But opening up to someone takes time. It can be a tough thing to do, so don't be afraid to go slow and let it build over time.

Heal Your Core Wounds
Chapter Ten: Dr. David B. Hawkins

When it comes to relationships, our past experiences can significantly impact our present connections. Anyone who has lived has past experiences. Some of them are good, some bad. What about you? Most of us have emotional wounds from our past. We call these Core Wounds. Let us explore what core wounds are and how to identify and heal them.

Core wounds originate from early traumatic experiences. Often rooted in childhood, they tend to resurface in adult relationships. These emotional wounds shape our beliefs about ourselves and others. These imprints continue to affect us into adulthood. They involve deep emotional pain that we suppress.

For instance, a core wound might make us feel unworthy or unlovable due to childhood trauma. We often discover, in our experiences while working with covert (vulnerable) narcissists, a history of trauma perpetrated by parents or guardians.

One thing to consider about core wounds is they can be helpful. They are often the instigator of empathy. As discussed earlier in the book, empathy is critical for caring for spouses and others with whom we are in close relationship.

It is obvious that a victim of any kind of abuse will have core wounds. The variety and intensity, though, of these wounds certainly depends on the destructive nature of the abuse. In addition, the depth of the core wounds experienced is likely to correlate to the length of time your victim has been subjected to abuse.

What may not be as obvious to the general public, is that narcissists have core wounds as well. In fact, their core wounds are often deeper than those of their victim(s).

The typical core wounds of a narcissist revolve around feelings of insecurity, low self-esteem, and – ironically – vulnerability. Because of a history lacking empathy, little or no encouragement, and shame or guilt, things narcissists crave, they do not know how to exhibit these life-enhancing attributes.

To complicate these struggles even more, the narcissist will project inadequacies onto their victim(s) to overcompensate for their own shortcomings. As a form of denial and protection, a narcissist will accuse their victim of abusive behavior(s) to deflect attention away from themselves. These accusations serve to protect the narcissist or emotional abuser.

In the following chapter, we will unveil a roadmap outlining several Core Emotional Wounds. We will learn how to identify them, and how to "heal" them. However, it is a long road to personal enlightenment. Because of this, it is likely that, at least initially, inviting a professional, knowledgeable counselor into the process is necessary.

Everyone who struggles with emotional wounds will need someone – hopefully a trained professional – to identify, understand, and heal core wounds. This cannot be overstated. The aid of an expert is critical to enhance the likelihood of recovering a healthy sense of self and overcoming the pain of core wounds. Navigating through the challenges of core wounds is neither a swift nor easy journey. To effectively manage the pain core wounds bring requires strong, healthy support.

If you are honest with yourself, you will acknowledge the importance of seeking help in addressing even the most straightforward issues. Doesn't it make sense that you should ask for assistance with more complex issues? Although getting support from a professionally trained counselor or therapist is a logical, healthy step you might believe you can "handle things" on your own.

Do you trust yourself more than you should? Often, it is pride that keeps you from seeking help when you really need it.

Why not admit the need for help? Is pride keeping you from voicing your limitations? Pride is often the biggest obstacle to overcoming difficulties in life. It prevents us from admitting a problem or asking for help when we need it. If you are too proud to admit the need for help, you are alone in your fight. Fighting alone rarely finds success.

As professionals will attest, attempting to work through core wounds alone is not likely to end with much, if any, progress. While recognizing your struggles is a good beginning; accurately identifying and naming specific wounds holding you back, and stifling your progress requires assistance. In the next section, we will present different types of core wounds and how each of these affects individuals differently.

Professional help can guide you through the process. Ultimately, the best help will come through the aid of a professional expert – especially one familiar with narcissism and emotional abuse.

Although you may have some temporary resolution and success when working independently, your best opportunity for substantial and sustainable change is with professional assistance. You can certainly educate yourself on the basics of core wounds and how to work through them, a thorough understanding of the genesis of your wounds, their impact on you, and how best to work through and overcome them can be gained by inviting an expert to speak into your life.

Types of Core Emotional Wounds include:

Shame wound: Feeling constantly ashamed due to past embarrassment. Being called out by parents or adults in your life growing up in harmful, guilt-ridden ways creates a wound of imbalance. Dumping shame on another person – when personal confidence has already been compromised – undermines an individual's ability to thrive. Later, you repeat what was modeled for you in your interactions with your spouse and children. Even though it is the last thing you want, you have become your parents, and this is destroying your wife and children.

There is a wounded part of you related to shame. This is often because you do not know how to relate concerns or problems in healthy ways. Furthermore, in a lot of individuals, this is because of your parent(s) acting out in dysfunctional ways.

Judgment wound: Carrying self-criticism from severe judgments. Did your parents or caregivers have high expectations for you? Were their expectations unrealistic? Perhaps those you most hoped for affirmation from were supercritical and judgmental. Judgment and condemnation will break a person's spirit, ultimately, destroying you.

Betrayal wound: Fear of being hurt by others due to betrayal. When you feel betrayed, more than just a trust being broken, the victim of the betrayal feels stabbed in the back at a moment when support is critically important. Being betrayed over and over tends to undermine your confidence. A history of betrayal leads a person to become a skeptic.

This can lead to an individual craving loyalty, the opposite of betrayal. But, because of so much historical betrayal, you might have come to a point where you are convinced that loyalty is a façade.

Rejection wound: Holding onto hurt from past dismissals. Everyone wants to be accepted. Repeated rejection is likely to convince you that nobody cares, much less loves you. This shows up across various levels and degrees of severity. Simple rejection tactics include dismissal and not listening to someone else's input or perspective.

On a more intense level, rejection can manifest as complete disregard such as completely ignoring someone altogether or never inviting your spouse into decision-making. Another form of this is a noticeable lack of emotional or physical affection.

Abandonment wound: Clinging to a relationship out of fear you will be left, stemming from early experiences of abandonment. An individual who feels abandoned loses trust in the loyalty needed in a relationship and eventually loses hope in anyone's ability to be loyal. As a reaction to this, the victim may become unapproachable – protecting themselves from harm – and preventing others from getting close enough to abandon them. By avoiding close connections, they avoid being hurt.

Understanding these distinct Core Wounds and how they most impact the individuals and the people around them is critical. With proper assistance, as mentioned earlier, these wounds can be identified sooner and more proactively addressed.

Identifying Core Wounds: Identifying core wounds is the beginning of your healing. Discovering and understanding your core wounds is a powerful step toward healing and personal growth. Here are some strategies to help you identify these emotional imprints:

Pause and Reflect: Take quiet moments to explore your feelings, reactions, and patterns. Here are some healthy questions to ask yourself:

What situations trigger intense emotions?

When do I feel most vulnerable or defensive?

Are there recurring themes in my relationships?

Asking these and other similar questions promotes the opportunity for you to better understand what emotions are most troubling to you. With this knowledge, you can better recognize times when you might become more susceptible or open to vulnerability.

Emotional Assessment: Regularly assess your personal emotional landscape. What emotions are prevalent? Are there consistent themes? Having a clear picture of what is going on in and around you – especially emotionally – is not just enlightening. A clear view gives you an edge. Clarity gives you the opportunity to turn your attitude and behavior in a positive direction. That is if you respond to this understanding well.

Adding to your insights through pauses and reflection, and engaging in emotional assessments, builds your understanding of how you might respond under specific circumstances in the future.

Journaling: Write down your thoughts and feelings.

Document your experiences and any memories that evoke strong emotions. Look for themes in your writing and present these concerns to those you trust.

Even if journaling feels unfamiliar or awkward for you, it is surprising how quickly it can become a habit. Start with jotting down 2-3 sentences about your day. Keep it simple at the beginning and just write down your general thoughts for how the day went.

Explore Childhood Memories

Early Experiences: Reflect on your upbringing. What were your family dynamics like? Were there significant events or traumas? If you experienced a close-knit family with memorable extended family get-togethers, it is more likely you will emphasize the need for close connections in your immediate family now. However, if your immediate family was distant or disconnected, these patterns may become realized in your new relationships.

Parental Influence: Consider how your parents or caregivers treated you. Were there moments of rejection, criticism, or neglect? Repeated long-term neglect or criticism severely impacts self-confidence and esteem. Rejection, also discussed earlier in this chapter, is the more powerful dismissal. If these were your experiences with your parents, then you might come across now as someone who seeks attention or craves excessive admiration.

Attachment Styles: Explore attachment theory. Did you feel secure, anxious, or avoidant in childhood relationships? The type of attachment you experienced during your early years has a great impact on your ability to connect with others as an adult.

A secure attachment instills confidence and trust that others care about you. If this is you, it is more likely you will have strong bonds with others and a loving, trusting relationship with your spouse.

An anxious attachment style is evidenced by a childhood history of non-existent or unloving parents. That unattached parent-child scenario creates uncertainty. Over time, as a child, you lose hope of a nurturing relationship with your parent(s) and seek attention elsewhere.

Finally, an avoidant attachment style often results in an adult who struggles to trust a marriage partner or develop close, intimate relationships. The avoidant person will usually prefer self-reliance and extreme independence – even to the point of refusing to share feelings with their spouse. You might even deny the need for emotional support or closeness.

Healing Core Wounds

Acknowledge the issue and accept there is a problem:
The first step in healing core wounds is recognizing you have wounds and examining your feelings and emotions related to them.

Suppressing them only prolongs the pain. As with most emotional challenges in life, we must reach a point where we are willing to acknowledge that there is a problem. Only then can efforts be made to address it.

Share your discoveries with self-reflection and compassion: Embrace vulnerability and expose buried pain. We should encourage each other to pursue self-reflection with open minds and hearts to better understand how these wounds impact your life and the lives of others. Doing this with compassion is necessary to convey care for yourself; and, more importantly for the people close to you.

Seek Healthy support: Lean on friends, family, therapists, and coaches. Allow yourself to be seen, received, and loved by others. As discussed, in-depth earlier in this chapter, it is often critical to enlist the aid of professionals promoting the healthiest support.

Inner Work: Practices like shadow work, inner child work, and mindfulness can aid healing. Chapters 6 and 8 – earlier in this book – present a more detailed review of these subjects.

Our shadow self exists in our negative traits. Because these are "shadows", we often cannot see them without the help of others. Shadow work is the effort to combine our conscious selves with the part of ourselves we tend to ignore or repress. Merging these two sides of ourselves is necessary for us to see both the good and bad and realize ourselves as complete beings.

Inner child work requires us to consider past experiences and their impact on us as adults. Some experiences can be so negatively severe that we have become trapped – subconsciously – at a younger age. The inner child, that which remains at an arrested age, does not function well as an adult. Just knowing we are stuck is only the beginning of this work. We need help to understand who we are, the changes that need to be accommodated, and how to "grow through" the stifled development.

Mindfulness, being keenly aware of how we are showing up and what we are reacting to in unhealthy ways, is critical for us to be able to see the need for acknowledging and addressing changes. Mindfulness is having an accurate understanding of, and naming, the uncomfortable emotions we have and adapting to the reality of our current experiences.

As you can now see, there are various ways for you to address core wounds associated with narcissism and emotional abuse. The goal is to utilize these methods and resources to overcome your personal challenges, thereby preventing tendencies to act out negatively or perpetrate similar behaviors towards your wife.

Remember, identifying and healing core wounds is an ongoing process. Healing core wounds will lead you to healthier, more fulfilling relationships. Be gentle with yourself and seek support. By unraveling these emotional knots, you pave the way for healthier relationships and personal transformation.

Embracing 360 Degree Feedback and Relapse Prevention

Chapter Eleven: Dr. David B. Hawkins

You've been called a narcissist. This book began by asking what you wanted to do about it. Now, as we reach the end of the book, we are going to ask again: What are you going to do about it? We expect you've given the issue a lot of thought and have decided you must change.

You were called a narcissist because you have been narcissistic and emotionally abusive. People were hurt by both your actions, and inactions. Unless you want things to continue as they have been going, you must change.

You must now admit this hard truth and stare change in the face. You've been called a narcissist. Get over it. Why have you been told you are selfish, mean and full of yourself? Because you are, and if you can't come to terms with that, you are going to lose a lot more than you've already lost.

Is this still hard to hear? Sure, but you need to hear this over and over if you are going to change. You may still have time to save what is precious to you, but not if you remain in denial.

This book is coming to a conclusion and at this juncture, it is critical to understand your work never ends. You have gained momentum as you've worked through the book and interacted with the different stories and various directions, but the book is at its end, and you need to keep it going.

The fact is it took a long time to become the way you are, and it will take significant work and tenacity to maintain the work. Going forward, remember the subtitle to this book: *doing the work to end patterns of narcissism and emotional abuse.*

The heart of this final chapter is quite simple: You must be vigilant and alert, at all times, embracing 360-degree feedback, watching for moments when you're taking steps forward and times when you are regressing.

You have read how to do this.

Maintaining Your Focus

Preparing to write this final chapter, I reflected on all the stories I've heard from men—stories of spectacular gains and devastating losses. The gains always came after long, hard, measured work and their losses came after lapses of focus, laziness, and recklessness. From here forward you cannot risk even a moment of recklessness, because time is not on your side. Do you understand that?

Progress, and recovery from narcissism and emotional abuse require being vigilant about that process. Your progress is similar to playing the game of Chutes and Ladders. You remember this game, where you roll the dice and pray you land on a ladder, taking you to the winner's circle, and avoiding the chutes, where you slide backwards. Only now, in this real game of your life—you choose when to 'climb a ladder' and 'when to slide backward.' It's not about the luck of the dice, but about responsible decision-making.

An important aspect of your decision-making, and your ongoing growth, involves reflection, feedback, and accountability. Socrates wisely said, "The unexamined life is not worth living." While this advice is true, we are not very good at following it. We're too often independent loners, determined to 'do our own thing,' often to our severe detriment. This must change. Focus!

Embracing Feedback

You've been called a narcissist for good reason. Why? You've listened to your own counsel and ignored the years of critical feedback you've been given from your mate. You've rebelled from invaluable direction, and it's cost your mate and you a lot. That's not going to work anymore.

It's time to embrace, not fight, feedback. Embracing feedback means letting go of pride, as we explored earlier in the book. It means critically examining your thoughts, your actions, and all the excuses you tell yourself for behaving the way you have behaved.

It's time to reflect and reconsider your life to determine your new approach. Reconsideration, however, cannot happen in an atmosphere where you hear only your own thoughts, again and again. You need new information. You must embrace 360-degree feedback.

Echo Chambers

Let's face it. You've been called a narcissist because you've pridefully clung to your ways of thinking and doing things. You've lived exclusively in what's been called '*an echo chamber*'--where you listen only to yourself or others around you who support your thinking. If you fail to obtain new information, your thoughts and attitudes will never be challenged.

Most of us say we want feedback, when we really don't. Most of us cling to our own well-rehearsed thoughts, and if we seek feedback at all, it is typically from people who agree with us.

We resist people who disagree with us.

Why is there such a disparity between what we say we want— feedback—and what we do—listen primarily to our own thinking? Even when we know feedback is good, why do we avoid it?

It boils down to this--- we want to do what we want to do. We're self-centered and immature. We don't really want someone to criticize our thinking. We don't really want someone to tell us we're doing it all wrong. It's too painful. If, after all, someone tells us we're heading in the wrong direction, and we listen, we must correct our course and that requires a change in attitude, thoughts, and direction. So, instead, we believe our own views, avoiding information that contradicts our thinking.

It is time to completely let go of denial and avoidance of tough issues. It's time to do the very hard work stop blaming others for your problems and embrace hard, challenging truths.

Defensive, Dismissive, Denial

You've been called a narcissist because you have denied what you're doing is wrong. You've been in massive denial. You must never forget this.

You can't sit with these lies any longer. They're hurting you and those you love. Remember, denial keeps you safe for the moment but slowly destroys your life. This mindset protects you for the moment but keeps you hopelessly stuck, and the consequences of your actions will have severe repercussions.

Johari Window

Have you recognized denial in your behavior? One very useful tool we teach in our Core Men's Group for confronting denial is the Johari Window. This is a powerful means for embracing feedback.

The Johari Window was developed in 1955 by two psychologists, Joseph Luft and Harry Ingham. ('Johari' is a combination of their names.) What these men discovered is there are areas of our lives known and open to others, areas known only to ourselves, areas known to others but not ourselves (blind spots), and areas unknown to both you and others.

It is important to recognize we may not be as open as we believe, and there is information others have about us that can be critically important. If we are open to it, others can share with us those things we don't fully know about ourselves.

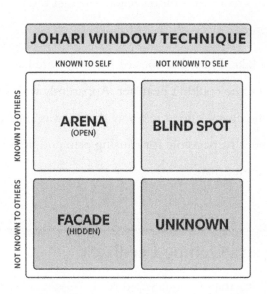

Jake has been a regular member of the Core Men's Group now for several weeks and is making consistent progress. He recently shared he'd decided to obtain feedback from his family on his progress—a brave and risky step. Specifically, he decided to ask what they liked about him, what they disliked about him, and what counsel they might give him for his personal growth.

"My son shared information that practically killed me. He told me things he'd wanted to tell me, (issues my wife, and his mother had been trying to share with me for years) but was afraid. He said I'm a braggart and don't follow my own advice. He assured me he loved me but said I was always right so he never liked he could share anything personal with me for fear of being told he was wrong. He was very nervous talking to me, but I listened and let his words sink in. It hurt like heck, and I had to really work at not defending myself. I listened. I didn't react. I just let the words sink in. It was powerful for me."

As I listened to Jake, I heard echoes of what his wife had shared with him months ago, but he couldn't hear her. Apparently with his work in the group, his son's feedback landed in a way that he was able to hear and now understands he is responsible for causing pain and he is going to make a change to be a better man.

Resisting Giving and Getting Feedback

Jake did something that was gutsy and really showed his growth. He courageously leaned into difficult feedback. He stifled his defensiveness and listened to the truth, which is very hard to do.

You must do the same.

You've been called a narcissist because you not only resist receiving feedback, but *you also resist even asking for it*. Going forward you must make it a habit to ask for critical feedback. You must check in with people who are important to you and invite critical feedback. This won't be easy. You'll be tempted to resist and avoid critical feedback. In the past, you've most likely made it impossible for your mate or children, to approach you.

You've been defensive, not only not inviting critical feedback but making it impossible for anyone to give you needed feedback without defending or counter-accusing. All of this must change.

You may be squirming at the thought of inviting criticism. I get it. Think about who you're ready to receive feedback from. Can you see the value of creating a healthy feedback loop?

The Value of Feedback

Feedback is life for all of us. Feedback is what allows us to grow. Can you see this? You cannot grow without it. We cannot see or reflect upon 'blind spots' and change without it.

Consider the specific value of feedback:

Feedback reinforces positive habits. With feedback we more clearly see what we are doing that is helpful and wholesome. Just as we need to 'see' what we do that is harmful, we must also 'see' what we're doing that is helpful to others.

Feedback builds self-awareness. Knowing we will be receiving feedback, we become watchful. We take note of our actions that are valued and take immediate reparation for those actions that are hurtful Feedback gives us the opportunity we learn more about ourselves and others, giving us space to grow in our self-awareness.

Feedback promotes empathy. Learning the impact we have on others; we have the opportunity to adjust our actions accordingly. We learn to listen to others and become more respectful and sensitive to them. We learn from our mistakes and our positive actions. Our awareness of others, subsequently, grows.

Feedback becomes a fundamental part of effective two-way communication. If you think of communication as a process of, give and take, with our actions always influencing others, we must always be watchful. We need real-time feedback to make critical adjustments. How is what I'm saying being received? How am I being impacted by what this person is saying to me?

Finally, feedback allows us to analyze the effect of our communication. When you think of a relationship as people impacting one another, you understand that continued feedback is essential to understanding how the relationship is doing.

Feedback then is vital. You always know where you stand in a relationship, knowing at any given moment how you are doing.

Value in Walking on Eggshells

Most believe 'walking on eggshells'---where we are extra cautious around another person-- to be detrimental. Think again. Walking on eggshells can be a very positive, reflective thing to always be doing.

Recently I had a man make this complaint:

"Now I feel like I'm walking on eggshells, just like my wife has said about herself. It's exhausting. How can this be healthy? I'm watching every word I say. I watch my wife for expressions of irritation and then I apologize. Sometimes I don't even get what

I'm apologizing for it. I can't live like this."

Another man in the group quickly jumped in.

"Actually, you *can* live like this. We all need to be 'on guard,' ready to make corrections. I've been messing up for a long time and it's time for me to be watching my step. There's no room left in my marriage for me to make any more mistakes."

Others in the group quickly agreed. Rather than being something negative, 'walking on eggshells' was now viewed as a very positive feeling. As you recalibrate your life, you will need to be extremely careful. Remember, you've caused so much harm you must take every precaution to stop any more harm. The feeling of 'walking on eggshells.' will be a good reminder of your commitment to change.

You may, for a time, feel like it's all unfair. But it's not at all. 'Walking on eggshells' is the price you pay for reconsidering your life. It's the price you pay for having an opportunity to restore your marriage if it's even possible. Having your actions scrutinized is the price you pay for what you've done.

Remember, no victims are allowed. You decide if you want to 'walk on eggshells.' For you not to feel resentful you must remind yourself you're choosing this path. You want to change, to grow, to live beyond your past. This requires embracing feedback.

The 5 Rs of Feedback

Gustavo Razzetti designed a brilliant model for embracing feedback. He says there are '5 R's' for giving and receiving feedback.

Request: *Taking the Initiative.* Unsolicited feedback often backfires so it is healthy to seek feedback. Be very clear with others about what kind of help you're looking for.

Receive: *Active Listening.* It is critical to be open to feedback given. Create a culture where giving and receiving feedback is the norm. Listen to the feedback and receive it non-defensively.

Reflect: *Gaining Insight.* Take time to reflect before reacting. Consider the validity of the feedback. Don't immediately discard the feedback, even if it feels inaccurate. See the feedback as a gift to ponder.

Respond: *Constructively Reply.* Let the feedback giver know you have spent time reflecting on their feedback and you value the energy they put into the process.

Resolve: *Commit to Grow.* After reflecting on the feedback, make a commitment to grow. Whether you totally accept the feedback is up to you, but you owe the person the respect of considering their feedback.

As you can see, learning to accept feedback is going to be a challenge. Practicing the 5 R's, however, will help you grow as a person.

Relapse Prevention

The last important task we must discuss before we close the book is the topic of *relapse prevention.* Progress, after all, is not worth much if it can't be maintained. Progress ceases to be progress when there is regression—so, you need to do everything possible to keep your progress moving forward.

Relapse prevention is where you create a concrete plan to keep your progress going and avoid lapses in progress. Relapse prevention requires you to create a strategy to avoid relapse.

1. Create a clear definition of what relapse looks like and what you're trying to avoid. Make this goal very specific.

    - Manage your emotions and avoid abusive eruptions.
    - Practice empathy and validating your mate.
    - Avoiding patterns of domination and defensiveness.

2. Identify triggers to your relapse behaviors.

    - Consider potential scenarios, thoughts, or feelings that might trigger a relapse
    - If triggered, rehearse how you will respond to avoid relapse.

3. Specify strategies used to cope with triggers.

    - Create a list of friends you might call.
    - Consider which tools will be most effective in this situation.
    - Soothe yourself such as journaling.

4. Who will support you in your Relapse Prevention plan?

    - Make a list of people who might act as Accountability Partners.
    - List the supportive people who understand your situation and want you to succeed

5. Prepare for the worst.
   - Imagine the worst happening, where you experience triggers and temptations to relapse into old, unwanted behaviors
   - Note how you will effectively cope
   - Stop, plan your escape
6. Track your progress honestly and make adjustments accordingly.
   - Be very candid with yourself about how your Relapse Prevention plan is working
7. reinforce what is working, revise what is not
8. *Finally,* get feedback on your plan.
   - Get feedback on your Relapse Prevention Plan
   - Utilize feedback for revising your plan

Take the time to map out a plan for maintaining your progress. Remember what I said—I've seen wonderful gains by men and devastating losses. The losses always occurred because the man was ill-prepared for the challenges he faced in recovery.

You will be challenged, your weak spots exposed. If you don't follow a solid plan of relapse prevention, anything you have gained can be lost in a moment. You've worked too hard to allow that to happen.

The Path Forward

Through doing the work in this book, you now understand why you were called a Narcissist. This is a critical admission. Being called a Narcissist, however, does not need to define you going forward. The skills taught throughout this book will help guide you into the next stage of your life. You are now poised and ready to begin living your life free from abuse and filled with healthy relationships.

We've explored together how letting go of denial and 'thinking errors' will make a huge difference. You've explored how attitudes of entitlement and selfishness will completely stall your progress. Moreover, you've embraced the importance of change— real, honest change.

Now, armed with humility, transparency and openness, are you prepared to keep your progress going? By continuing the work, by making real changes, you are inviting your mate and the people you care about to share with you a healthy and loving relationship.

Seven Common Questions Men in Treatment Ask

Throughout this book, we've attempted to address the major issues we see men face. However, no matter how much material is written, there are always questions. We always have questions and that's a good sign because it indicates you are thinking, considering, and reflecting on the issues covered in this book.

Therefore, we've chosen to tackle some of the frequent questions we hear from men working with us at the Marriage Recovery Center and The Emotional Abuse Institute. The following pages will address questions you may encounter during your personal journey as you take ownership of your history of emotional abuse. We know nothing is straightforward, but we hope you find answers here to some of your ongoing questions.

Does therapy really have to take a long time?

The short answer to this question is 'yes.' Making changes to the character, which is typically needed for issues involving emotional abuse, is not simple. If we were simply talking about learning a technique like managing anxiety or learning some communication skills, this might be an issue of shorter duration. But when we're talking about changing an attitude, as well as deeply entrenched patterns of acting and thinking, the process is longer.

Keep in mind that therapy becomes even longer and more challenging due to the issue of denial. Men in the Core program learn 'you can't change what you don't own,' and simultaneously learn to recognize the many ways they defensively maneuver to avoid owning their destructive patterns. Men learn that the very thoughts and actions they use to protect themselves (denial) make treatment all the more difficult.

Men in treatment discover, usually very slowly, that they have caused more harm to their mate than they believed, or that they want to admit, causing treatment to be a 'two steps forward, one step back' process. The issue of 'ownership,' a foundational principle of treatment, is more difficult than they initially expected.

Another factor making treatment more challenging is the issue of avoiding feeling shame and remorse. Most men in our programs are 'shame sensitive,' meaning they are hyper-sensitive to feeling shame. They feel shamed and 'attacked' when no attack is present. They often recoil in the face of feeling criticized and, unless they are very careful, may react, making matters worse.

So, does treatment have to be long and involved? Probably. The men in our treatment program are, for the most part, hardworking men. Yet, they come to treatment late in the game, having caused a lot of harm to them. Keep in mind that therapy becomes even longer and more challenging due to the issue of denial. others and have deeply entrenched character patterns. Therefore, the best thing to do is be at peace with however long treatment takes and appreciate the good things that come from positive change. Therapy is not a punishment, but an opportunity to 'grow up.'

Shouldn't therapy be a 'two-way street'?

No! While it is common to want to 'equalize' the problems, making us feel better, equal apportionment of problems is not a healthy way to think about issues when it comes to narcissistic and emotional abuse.

Does she have problems? Possibly. Has she contributed to some of the marriage problems? Possibly, again. However, there is no growth for you if you spend your time and effort comparing issues and assigning responsibility for who brought what issue into the relationship. When it comes to abuse, the medical term "triage" comes to mind. Triage is the process used to determine the priority of patients' treatments based on the severity of their condition

What this means when we look at abuse is: that there is greater weight given to your issues since your actions are harmful to her personhood. Emotional abuse is not a common communication problem. It's much more serious than that. Emotional abuse diminishes another's well-being. It robs the victim of their safety, degrading and robbing them of their liveliness.

It is critical for men in our treatment groups to let go of the 'two-way street' mentality, to not get caught up in things being equal to be fair. There is no injustice since you've largely created this situation.

We encourage the men to focus solely on themselves and change what they can change, knowing that in time, if they do their work, they very well may get the opportunity to talk about issues of mutual concern. Until then it is critical to focus solely on the harm they have caused and on growing their character.

What if I believe I've changed, and she doesn't see it?

This is a common problem, to be sure. What we notice is when there have been years of narcissistic and emotional abuse, it takes a long time not only for a change to occur, but for that change to be noticed and felt.

Step back and consider her perspective. She has felt violated and betrayed for years and has repeatedly voiced her complaints about mistreatment. That is her reality. By the time she has fully acknowledged the extent of the harm done to her, significant damage has already been done. Men who are in the early stages of the change process cannot expect her to immediately recognize or trust these changes. Rather, they need to be patient and let their positive actions demonstrate their commitment.

In the spirit of 'two steps forward, one back,' it is common for the victim of emotional abuse to feel very discouraged at the step backward. Even though progress is truly being made, she will feel the weight of the misstep far more than the progressive steps. The man must be patient and allow her to feel her discouragement.

Another mistake many men make is to 'toot their own horn.' When she doesn't notice his progress, he mistakenly calls her attention to the progress he has made. This never goes well. She needs to see and experience the changes on her own, rather than have him point out his progress.

So, the men in treatment need to stick with it, knowing that in time she will notice the positive changes. It won't happen as quickly as he would like, but it will happen.

What if my wife has a double standard?

It can be very frustrating when we sense someone has a double standard. How is it fair to have one standard for you and another for her? It would seem that a guideline should work both ways. This, however, is not necessarily the case.

Double standards happen and there's not much to do about it. We know that's not the answer you want. I'm sure you would prefer that the rules you are being asked to follow apply to her as well.

Remember what we said about 'cleaning your side of the street' and keeping your sole focus on you? That is the only thing you can control.

Additionally, we've found that even trying to 'make things fair' invariably backfires. She will resent you for trying to apply what you've learned to her. She already has a long history of feeling controlled and any efforts you make to make matters 'even' will only add fuel to her fire. Don't do it. Let it go.

Can I share what I'm learning with her?

This is a matter best considered on a case-by-case basis. Some mates want to know all about what you're learning in your treatment and want to see you applying it to your daily life. Most, however, want to know what you are learning only as long as it applies to you. Not as a method of weaponizing her.

Remember that she has been victimized by you. She has been controlled and manipulated and has her radar up on these matters. If you try to teach her what you are learning, it will undoubtedly backfire. You are not the teacher---you're the student.

Take your learning and apply it to you. You become a better person and lead by example. You can teach her a lot by giving her what has been called a 'corrective emotional experience.' This means as she experiences you in a healthy way, one day she will come to fully appreciate your changes.

Why can't it be that I'm just a normal guy with normal problems?

Because that is not what this is. If you were 'a normal guy with normal problems,' you wouldn't need extensive treatment to change. If this was an everyday problem requiring you to read a book and have six weeks of counseling, there would be no need for extensive treatment.

Sadly, the issues of narcissism and emotional abuse are far more complex than that.

We know men genuinely wrestle with this issue, which is why we titled our book and hence the title of our book: So, You've Been Called a Narcissist. Now what? We understand labels can be and it takes significant effort to move beyond the sting of being labeled. However, we also recognize that accepting the situation is a huge step toward healing.

Does this mean you're abnormal? No, what it means is that your character issues have extended beyond being simple, everyday problems. It means that self-will is no longer effective. It means specialized treatment is needed and if you participate fully in treatment, you will make significant gains. Character change is possible for those who take treatment seriously.

One more thing: participating in this work doesn't mean you must walk around announcing to everyone that you're an emotional abuser. There are areas of your life where presumably you function normally. You and your therapist will need to determine the extensiveness of your issues and how much treatment you'll need.

When will things go back to the way they were in my marriage?

We've got both good news and bad news for you. Things will probably never go back to the way they were—and that's actually good news. This crisis is an incredible opportunity to reevaluate your life, critically reviewing all that's transpired to get you to this point.

Think about it. Your mate will likely never go back to where she was since that was a painful place for her. Hopefully, you don't want her to go back there. In fact, she will be hyper-alert to anything that even smacks of her old life. Change is drastically needed.

As for you, she's hoping you have no intention of going back to the way things were. She needs to know you are committed to being a healthy man and will be vigilant to guard against relapse.

Now, this doesn't in any way mean you cannot recreate a loving, healthy, and connected relationship, one you hopefully had some time ago. It doesn't mean you can't recreate a playful, joyful, and exciting relationship. That is fully possible. We have found that most women are resilient and want a healthy connection again.

They just don't want the abuse. They won't settle for their old life.

Again, change must occur.

Now, a word of caution. Far too often men want to put a Band-Aid on a major problem, rushing back to their old life and making only cosmetic changes. Their desire to resume some kind of normalcy short-circuits the change process and harms her more. They take shortcuts, wanting affirmation for minor efforts, encouragement for minimal change. They want forgiveness when the abuse continues. This is not a recipe for growth.

So, don't rush back to the way things were. Don't short-circuit the change process. Demand more for yourself, your marriage, and of course, her. Stop at nothing to bring about radical change to ensure you are becoming a healthy man.

COMPREHENSIVE CORE PROGRAM FOR MEN

Congratulations! You've taken a momentous step towards becoming a healthier you. Now it's time to put into practice what you've learned. Information is power, but only if it is coupled with action. If you are ready to take the next step, we invite you to join the Comprehensive Core.

The Comprehensive Core offers live teaching and coaching from a team of clinicians, including co-authors Dr. John Hudson, Dr. David Hawkins, and their team of trained clinicians. Alongside a small group of other men, you will forge new bonds and discover that you are not alone in this journey!

Together, you will break free of the cycle of shame, frustration, and destructive patterns. You will learn to identify and take ownership of the problematic behaviors that are sabotaging your life and your relationships. You will gain new skills to manage your emotions, understand the needs and emotions of your mate, and create pathways to connection. More importantly, you will be encouraged to practice your newfound skills in real-life scenarios, learn from your own mistakes and each other, and be part of an accountability group – the 3 keys to long-term change.

Join the hundreds of other men who have experienced life change and register for a **Comprehensive Core group**.

Visit marriagerecoverycenter.com/the-core

or call (206) 219-0145

Made in the USA
Monee, IL
05 December 2024

72610872R00125